Praise for *Women i*

"Nothing in God's word is superfluous. There are no by-the-ways," writes Betty Hamblen in her new work, *Women in the Shadows*. With insights gleaned through years as a professional counselor, language skills honed from teaching English and literature, and, most importantly, a very evident love for God and His teachings, Hamblen paints for us vivid portraits of 12 unnamed women in scripture. Believing "every account in the Bible is important," she shines a light on those often overlooked—from Jephthah's daughter in Judges 11 to the woman of Tekoa in 2 Samuel 14 to Pilate's wife in Matthew 27—and draws very specific and timely lessons we can learn from each. Ideal for personal study or for discussions in the classroom setting, I highly recommend this work from one of my favorite mentors!

— Teddy Copeland, Author of *SIT BY ME*
and other ladies' class books

When Betty shared the title and subject for her book, I was immediately intrigued. We know that God had a purpose for these women in the shadows and He gave us just enough detail. How clever of Betty to present a potential personal glimpse into the lives, struggles, and emotions of these women. I would love to study this book with a book club or a ladies' Bible class.

— Cindy Bright, Children's Bible Teacher

From the moment I started reading I couldn't put this book down!

It is short enough to read in one sitting, but beware! You'll go back to it again and again to gain more awareness of, and appreciation for, these 12 women. Betty's insights fascinated me, made me think about these Biblical women in new ways and sent me back to my Bible to study more.

This would be a wonderful guide for a class or Ladies Day . . . it's a must-read!

— Debbie May, Former Heritage Christian
University Board member


"Betty gives us a glimpse into the biblical world of unnamed but important women who made choices that affected outcomes of different but important people. We can learn lessons from the choices they made and hopefully make better ones. An interesting book from beginning to end, it definitely makes you think and wonder how you would act in those circumstances."

— Church Ladies' Book Club , Wichita, KS


An insightful look at the impact and lessons we can glean from some of the unnamed women of the Bible as recounted from the lens of a seasoned counselor's eyes. Definitely a must read this year!

— Karen Thompson RN, CHC Author of
*Heart and Soul* by Publishing Design

Betty brings God's word to life by helping us to see these *Women in the Shadows*. By bringing these women to light and exploring their lives, she helps us to see what we can learn from these very different women and how we can apply what we learn to our lives. This book will help you have a deeper understanding and, more importantly, a love of God's word and His message to us.

— Donna Curran, Women's Bible Teacher

"Betty does an incredible job of adding context to the scripture text of 12 women we read about in the Bible. I have often wondered about women in the Bible and their role in the story God wants us to hear. Betty not only shares her own insight into these women, but she presents the reader with insightful questions that help us understand how their story can affect our own reasonings about life and bring light to experiences we have already experienced or may be in the middle of.

Betty does not mince words and presents the scripture as fact, just as we read it from the word of God. In a world filled with political correctness, we see, through her narrative, topics we often want to skim over. Something we cannot afford to do as we live our journey to heaven."

— Lori Rankin, Senior Software Consultant

*Women in the Shadows* is precisely the Bible study I've needed—a balm for my soul and a challenge for my spirit. Each woman represented in this book is treated with careful attention, giving the reader a powerful glimpse into her personality and her place within the Scriptures. Hamblen's vibrant storytelling, wise treatment of the text, and practical applications brought these women's stories to life in a uniquely compelling way. I wept along with some, cheered along with others, and I was impacted by them all. For every woman seeking to enrich her spiritual walk, *Women in the Shadows* is a must-read.

— Lori Tays, Vice President, Mars Hill Bible School

# Women in the Shadows

Betty Hamblen

CYPRESS

Published by Cypress Publications

Manufactured in the United States of America

Cataloging-in-Publication Data

Hamblen, Betty, 1942–

Women in the shadows.

Includes Scripture index.

1. Bible—Biography. 2. Women in the Bible. I. Hamblen, Betty, 1942–. II. Title.

220.92 DDC20

ISBN: 978-1-956811-31-5 (paperback); 978-1-965811-32-2 (ebook).

LCCN: 2022915340

Cover design by Ginger Leigh.

For information:

Cypress Publications
3625 Helton Drive
PO Box HCU
Florence, AL 35630

www.hcu.edu/publications

*This book is dedicated to
all the women who, through their living faith in God,
have had such a powerful influence
on my life and the lives of countless others.*

# Acknowledgments

**Abundant gratitude to:**

The women's classes at Oakland Church of Christ (Florence, AL) and South Emporia Avenue Church of Christ (Wichita, KS) for studying through the first basic lessons that, years later, resulted in this book.

Cheryl Newton, Donna Curran, and Cindy Bright for reading the first chapters of the initial manuscript and giving on-target suggestions that improved the content.

The writers of the blurbs that appear in or on this book. You are the best!

My daughter, Monica, for diligently proofreading each chapter to spot misplaced commas, iffy words, and cloudy sentences. An invaluable service to a writer!

My daughter, Ginger, for using her abundant creativity to design a cover that fit precisely with my own non-creative and vague description.

My husband, Willie, for patiently listening to me read aloud each chapter, asking questions, and making comments that kept me focused and true to the Word.

For the memories of Nina, Lola, Lorene, Erlene, Mary Helen, and Dot and for the continuing presence of Virginia Ann and Glenda. All of them were and are strong, good women who have loved me, led me, and live daily in my heart and in my writings.

Dr. Bill Bagents, Jamie Cox, and Brad McKinnon of

Cypress Press for answering numerous questions with kindness and for giving encouragement in abundance.

# Contents

Bible Abbreviations    xiii

Introduction    xix

1. The Despairing Woman    1
2. The Disobedient Woman    10
3. The Conniving Woman    17
4. The Resolute Young Woman    25
5. The Otherworldly Woman    35
6. The Dramatic Woman    41
7. The Self-Sacrificing Woman    50
8. The Hospitable Woman    57
9. The Chronically Ill Woman    65
10. The Humble Woman    72
11. The Sinful Woman    80
12. The Fearful Woman    88
13. Final Thoughts    96

Notes    103

Bibliography    107

Scripture Index    113

About the Author    118

Also by Cypress Publications    120

Heritage Christian University Press    122

# Bible Abbreviations

## Old Testament

| | |
|---|---|
| Gen | Genesis |
| Exod | Exodus |
| Lev | Leviticus |
| Num | Numbers |
| Deut | Deuteronomy |
| Josh | Joshua |
| Judg | Judges |
| Ruth | Ruth |
| 1–2 Sam | 1–2 Samuel |
| 1–2 Kgs | 1–2 Kings |
| 1–2 Chr | 1–2 Chronicles |
| Ezra | Ezra |
| Neh | Nehemiah |
| Esth | Esther |
| Job | Job |
| Ps | Psalms |
| Prov | Proverbs |
| Eccl | Ecclesiastes |
| Song | Song of Solomon |

| | |
|---|---|
| Isa | Isaiah |
| Jer | Jeremiah |
| Lam | Lamentations |
| Ezek | Ezekiel |
| Dan | Daniel |
| Hos | Hosea |
| Joel | Joel |
| Amos | Amos |
| Obad | Obadiah |
| Jonah | Jonah |
| Mic | Micah |
| Nah | Nahum |
| Hab | Habakkuk |
| Zeph | Zephaniah |
| Hag | Haggai |
| Zech | Zechariah |
| Mal | Malachi |

## New Testament

| | |
|---|---|
| Matt | Matthew |
| Mark | Mark |
| Luke | Luke |
| John | John |
| Acts | Acts |
| Rom | Romans |
| 1–2 Cor | 1–2 Corinthians |
| Gal | Galatians |
| Eph | Ephesians |
| Phil | Philippians |
| Col | Colossians |
| 1–2 Thess | 1–2 Thessalonians |
| 1–2 Tim | 1–2 Timothy |
| Titus | Titus |
| Phlm | Philemon |
| Heb | Hebrews |
| Jas | James |
| 1–2 Pet | 1–2 Peter |
| 1–2–3 John | 1–2–3 John |
| Jude | Jude |
| Rev | Revelation |

# Women in the Shadows

# Introduction

A fleeting glimpse. That's all I saw before she slipped back into the shadows. But that one brief appearance was enough to fire my imagination and create a desire to know more about her.

I saw her early one morning as I was reading from chapter 27 of the gospel of Matthew. That chapter details Jesus's appearance before Pilate, the Roman governor of Palestine. Suddenly in verse 19 I caught a glimpse of the wife of Pilate. Her intense focused plea sent to her husband grabbed my heart. She and her words appear only in that one verse in the scriptures, and I longed to know more about her.

I wondered how she knew about "that righteous man" Jesus. Had they met? Had a trusted servant told her about seeing him heal the sick? Did she see him from an upper window as he rode into Jerusalem on a donkey? Was she watching furtively behind a screen as his accusers brought him before her powerful husband? Was she a follower of God?

I also wondered what her emotions might have been on that fateful day. What did she mean by being "greatly troubled" in a dream about Jesus? Did she believe she was clair-voyant and had functioned in that role previously? How did she react to having her plea ignored by her husband? What were her feelings when she heard about the crucifixion of "that righteous man"? Or did she witness that horrible death? Of course, I could then, and can now, only speculate about the answers to my questions. She is truly a woman in the shadows, but one that is linked forever to the most profound event in history.

During that early morning study, I also wondered why the Holy Spirit inspired Matthew to include this concise glimpse of a nameless woman known only by her marriage relation-ship. I then recalled accounts of other women in the Bible who were not named but whose words or actions were recorded by inspired writers. Believing that every account in the Bible is important, I began to research those women whose brief appearances are included in the living Word of God. It has been a rich and vibrant educational process for me, and I want to share some of what I have learned. I hope you enjoy the study as much as I have.

As you read, and discuss (if you are studying this in a class), please note the following:

- While they are in the shadows, the women included in this study were real. They worked at tasks suitable for their times and positions. They enjoyed relationships both good and bad. They experienced the same emotions that women in any time period do. Clothes, language, and culture may be different, but we share many feminine traits and experiences with them.
- The only facts about the women that I know are absolutely true are those that the Bible records. All other statements about them have come either

from records written by others or from my own suppositions formed after intense study from various sources.

- The scenes written in *italics* to begin each lesson are mine only. They are my imaginings of possible actions and thoughts of that one woman in that specific time under those particular circumstances. Please keep that in mind as you read those sections.

- I sincerely believe that every verse in the scriptures is included, not by chance, but on purpose. So, as you read the scripture text for these lessons, try to read with "new eyes." Ask yourself questions about the account. If you have access, read from various Bible translations and from commentaries to get a broader understanding. You might even look up words or phrases in the original Hebrew or Greek.

- Because I believe that God put into the scriptures exactly what we need, I have looked at each account of a shadow woman with this question: What does God want me to learn from her? I pray that will be your question, also. You may have answers other than the ones I have included in each lesson. If you do, I hope you will let me know about them. The Bible is loaded with rich nuggets that we can mine forever, and I long to dig deeper and find more.

By shining a light into the shadows, I hope you will see real women with real problems who made real choices. Sometimes their choices of words or actions brought them closer to God, and sometimes they led the women farther away from Him. Sounds very much like us, doesn't it?

One of the most potent arguments for truthfulness of the

scriptures is that God never put a "spin" on any account in the Bible. He included both the good and the bad, and oftentimes, even the ugly. Such are the accounts of these women in the shadows.

# Chapter 1

## *The Despairing Woman*

### Scripture Text: Job 1–2:10

*She knelt among the rugs in the tent, her head bowed almost to her knees. The words would not come. She opened and then blinked her eyes at the early morning light peeking over the jagged hill and piercing the curtained doorway. Although she had hurled thousands of words toward the heavens during the long, heavy days and nights, she now could not call up any of them. Sighing deeply, she wondered why it mattered anyway. Her pleas had done no good. Nothing changed, except to worsen.*

*"How quiet it is!" she thought as she had every day for months. There was no bleating of sheep, no snorting of camels, no shouts from drovers moving herds to more fertile grazing lands. There was just silence. Even the soft talk and giggles of female servants moving about their chores in the camp was gone. The few remaining servants went about their tasks with long, sad faces, missing all the others with whom they once toiled and laughed and lived. She thought bitterly, "And where are all those men that used to crowd around my husband to seek his advice?" Now, there was no one except three men whose words weighed heavily on her husband. The silence loomed.*

*For the hundredth time, she thought that she could adjust to the quietness of absent herds, servants, and men of the city if she could only hear the sweet, loving conversations of her children. But they were gone, too. All of them. All those strong, handsome young men and their three beautiful sisters, voices and smiles and laughter stilled in one tragic moment of one horrible day.*

*She shook her head as if to shake the thoughts from it. If she continued to think about the absence of her children, she knew she would lie down among the rugs, close her eyes, and die. But she couldn't, for what would happen to her husband? Even now, she could hear the painful moaning as he lay on the bed in his tent, turning to ease the pain. She rose, her joints stiff as a shepherd's staff, to offer him a little food and to take a cloth dipped in cool water to soothe his skin.*

* * *

## Tragedy

Job's wife. A word picture of deepest grief and despair. Has any one of us even come close to experiencing the life-changing losses that she and her husband suffered in the brief moments of one day? Their 500 yoke of oxen and 500 donkeys were captured by enemies who slaughtered the attending servants. All of their 7,000 sheep along with the shepherds were burned alive. And all of their 3,000 camels were captured by raiding parties of another enemy who also killed the herdsmen. The news of each loss was delivered by a lone surviving servant who did not finish speaking before another surviving servant delivered his message, followed quickly by another servant delivering a third shocking message.

## The Cruelest Strike

Three horrendous blows delivered in minutes of one brief day took away their possessions, income, food, and servants. But Satan the Destroyer was not finished. Before his victims could catch a breath, he delivered the cruelest of all the blows. Ten children, birthed, nurtured, loved, and prayed over by their parents, were gone in an instant, crushed in the collapse of a building while they were gathered around a table, eating and laughing together.

As a mother, even writing this leads me to weep. Surely the death of a child must be the foremost loss for a parent. And for Job's wife, whose identity and much of her purpose as a woman of her time was tied to motherhood, this must have seemed an insurmountable loss.

In seconds, her hopes for future generations were dashed. Her dreams of teaching grandchildren about their family history died in the crush of a building. The ponderings of her heart about guiding her offspring in devotion to God were snuffed out by Satan. Tragedy, grief, despair.

## Life Changes

The sudden changes that must have come for this woman and her husband as a result of the tragedies truly tax the mind. Job and his wife were cast suddenly from the highest level of their society to poverty, from respectability and friendships to isolation, and from a full house of children and a life full of tasks and responsibilities to emptiness. The intensity of grief endured by someone who has lost almost everything important to them is difficult to imagine.

Job's wife had few things left to her. She had her husband, and they both seemed to have good physical health. They also had a few servants who escaped from the disasters or were at

home in her household when the disasters occurred, but then
... Satan struck again.

In another cruel blow, Job lost his good health. Scholars
are not certain what kind of illness he had, but chapters 2, 7,
and 19 contain descriptions of the physical results. Job was
covered with sores from head to toe, he had no rest, his skin
hardened and then broke out, his breath was "strange," he was
"skin and bones," and he was isolated and groaning. His
illness was so painful he even used a sharp piece of pottery to
scrape his skin trying to find relief. This illness must indeed
have been difficult for Job's wife as she heard the only
remaining loved one in her household groan in his misery and
try to find any kind of momentary relief from pain.

## Brokenness

Have you ever felt so broken by life's circumstances that you
were overwhelmed?   If so, what were your emotions and
actions then?  Did you "go crazy" for a while? Did you lash
out? Did you say something hurtful, painful or wounding?
Something, that hours or days later, made you wish you had
snatched the words out of the air and stuffed them back in
your mouth before they became weapons? If you did, then
you may empathize with this shadow woman whose electri-
fying words echo through the thousands of years since she
said them.

The only time this woman moves from the shadows is
when she reacts to her husband's illness. After days (weeks?
months? years?) of his suffering, she tells Job to get rid of the
only thing that is holding him together, his integrity based on
his relationship with God. She tells him to curse (renounce)
God and die.

After reading Leviticus 24:13-16; Job 1:5, 11; 2:3-5, explain
why her statements are particularly grievous. As much as you

can, put yourself in her shoes. What do you think was her motivation for making such statements? Exhaustion, despair, grief, hopelessness?

Read carefully Job's reply to his wife in verse 10. Even though he might have been shocked by her words, notice that he does not call her a foolish woman. He offers a much kinder and gentler reply. He says only that she talks *like* a foolish woman.

How would a foolish woman talk? Would she number only life's losses but not the blessings? Would she strike out from her own deeply pained heart to discourage another? Would she speak only from a physical view of life and ignore the spiritual? The answer, of course, is yes. A foolish woman would do that.

## Differing Views of God

A.W. Tozer states that "the most portentous fact about any man is ... what he in his deep heart conceives God to be like."[1] He further notes that the base of idolatry "is the entertainment of thoughts about God that are unworthy of Him."[2]

If that is so, then how would you contrast the differing concepts of God that Job and his wife had? Would you note that Job's wife seemed to view God as good only when He was blessing them with good things? Or that she may have thought God was distant, and perhaps even punishing them, when bad things happened in their lives? Or that God was present with them through all the good times, but she could not find Him when they passed through the valleys of the shadow of death. Of course, we do not know what she thought; we only know her action as she lashed out at Job but really at God.

Although Job was not patient nor unquestioning, he seemed to see God as good all the time, no matter what happened in their lives. That God still cared for them and was present even when bad things happened. He reminded his wife that they had received good things from God. In his view, it was only reasonable then that they would also be recipients of troubles and ills.

Job understood the big picture of life, but his wife's view was limited by emotional pain. She only wanted relief, even if it was death, her husband's and her own.

## The Later Years

I would like to think that Job's wife heard what her husband said and answered with, "Yes, of course, you are right." I would like to know that she was penitent and fell on her knees before God asking his forgiveness and expressing her faith. I would like to think that she had a renewal of heart and spirit, but the scriptures are silent about that.

We are not told how long they both suffered. It could have been years. Emotionally draining and physically challenging years. But then we read chapter 42. Job's integrity and faith mattered. His endurance and trust had results. The Lord blessed the latter part of Job's life and, by extension, his wife's life.

In mercy and love for Job's faithfulness, God showered blessings on them again. God restored Job's fortunes. He even doubled their possessions and blessed them with another 10 children (42:10–17). Because of God's goodness, Job and his wife once again had light and life in their home.

## Closing Thoughts

The account of this woman in the shadows seems to show us two different reactions people can have to intense suffering, perhaps because of their differing concepts of God. Job argued with God, he called out to Him in his pain, and he listened to the answers God gave him. Although Job was not patient nor quiet about the losses and sorrows Satan had brought upon him, he was unwavering in his faith that God was good and could be trusted.

His wife, on the other hand, allowed grief over the losses (and no one argues about their significance) to overwhelm her. Unlike her husband, however, she did not appear to be experiencing the presence of God during her intense suffering, although He was there. Perhaps she did not cry to Him in her sorrow, or argue the unfairness of the tragedies, or ask Him for answers, or question Him, as Job did. She just wanted relief at any price from her pain. Her faith seems to have been swamped by the misery she felt at the moment.

## What Can I Learn from
## The Despairing Woman?

About facing hard times in my life? (See Ps 56:3, 4 and 1 Pet 5:6, 7)

About blessings that can come from suffering? (See Ps 119:67, 71; 2 Cor 1:8–10)

About what I can do when others are suffering? (See 1 John 3:18 and 2 Cor 1:3, 4)

* * *

### To Think About

Do you know someone who is suffering from grief or illness? Think carefully about what would be truly helpful and encouraging to that particular person and reach out to him or her.

Some people find it difficult to listen for God's voice during hard times. To make it easier for you, commit to memory one or more of the verses cited above about suffering or one from elsewhere in the scriptures. If you do so, it will be easier to recall when you need encouragement or when you need to encourage someone else. (*Ex: One of my favorites is Ps 34:17–19.*)

What is your concept of God? What do you think is the concept of God for most people in our culture? Write here or in a private notebook a short description of God as you conceive of Him.


Has your concept of God helped you in difficult times?

# Chapter 2

## The Disobedient Woman

**Scripture Text: Genesis 19**

*She muttered as she moved along the road to Zoar. "'Hurry, hurry, hurry!' they said. 'Then, when we did not move fast enough, they pulled us out the door!" Noting the others moving farther away, she quickened the pace.*

*"Zoar! I cannot believe Lot asked for us to go to Zoar! Zoar is not a real city—not like Sodom at all." She sighed, "But at least we will not be in the hills sleeping under a tree or in a cave!" Tears welled up as she imagined her beautiful daughters sleeping in a cold, damp cave among skittering creatures of the night. Then she shuddered as she remembered her husband's plea directed to the men of the city and their violent demands. "Take my daughters!" he had shouted. Fresh tears sprang up as she thought about what could have happened.*

*Her thoughts were as scattered as the pebbles under her feet that sprayed to the path side. She thought about the two men, claiming to have been "sent by God," who would carry out the destruction. "Oh, Sodom, they told us you would be punished, that you would be destroyed!" She stumbled slightly as she thought about her house being demolished. Her home, with all the beautiful things they had gathered through the years, crumbling into nothing? The men did not give them time to gather any belongings. "I certainly needed sandals with thicker soles!" she thought as she regained her footing.*

*The distance between her and the others widened. They seemed to scurry as quickly as rabbits. She stopped to catch her breath and was startled as suddenly the sky lit up as if on fire. "Oh, what is that?!" she cried, covering her ears against the abrupt, deafening noises. The explosive sounds and thuds of burning objects hitting so close were terrifying. She heard screams and loud cries from behind her! Her heart pounded like a hammer on an anvil.*

*She then remembered the men's warning not to look back or stop, but Sodom was where her friends and home were. "My life is there!" she cried as she turned.*

\* \* \*

WARNING! Contains incidents of proposed abuse of women and homosexuality, violence, incestuous relationships and deathly destruction.

If you saw that alert for a movie you had selected to watch on television, you might immediately hit the "off" button. But that is exactly what the biblical account of this woman in the shadows contains.

Lot's wife and family lived in the wicked city of Sodom. If some of us lived in a place as evil as Sodom had become, we might be posting a "House for Sale" sign soon. But Lot and his wife and children were not looking to move. They continued to live in Sodom, the place Lot had chosen because it looked rich and well-watered (Gen 13:10–13).

Looks, however, can be deceiving, and we humans have limited vision. God saw reality. The inhabitants were "wicked, great sinners against the Lord."

## Life in Sodom

What do you suppose life was like for Lot's wife in a city such as Sodom? Remember that Lot and his wife were wealthy. Lot (and perhaps his wife) had lived and journeyed with his uncle Abram, a pillar of faith. They worshipped the one true God, offering praise and thanksgiving at the altars Abram had built (Gen 12:4–9). So, they had a lot of possessions, and they were God worshippers. Would life be easy for them in Sodom?

To understand more about what life was like in Sodom, read Ezekiel 16:49–50 and note the six characteristics and actions recorded about the city. How do you think each of those would affect people of God living in the midst of the city? Do you think she had difficulty finding a social group? If she found one, do you think the group of women would gossip, be exclusive, and attack each other, making her extremely uncomfortable? In what other ways might pride, haughtiness, and ease influence social life for Lot's wife? What is the likelihood that she was influenced by those around her and became proud and haughty herself?

A godly family in Sodom must have found it nearly impossible to rear their children in the Lord. Have you ever heard a child say, "But everybody's doing it! Why can't I?" In Sodom it may have been true that everybody was doing it, whatever sinful activity "it" might have been.

Being parents of daughters in that time period meant finding prospective grooms for them. Our text indicates that Lot and his wife had found men from Sodom who became betrothed to their two daughters, but notice verse 4 in our text. That passage indicates that *all* the men of Sodom surrounded Lot's house demanding that his male guests be brought out for their perverted use. Were the future sons-in-law among them? If so, how comforting would that be to a godly parent's heart?

If Lot's wife openly tried to live righteously, I wonder if neighbors scoffed at her. Have you ever been called "self-righteous" because you tried to live morally? If you are studying this lesson in a class setting, and are comfortable doing so, discuss with the class an incident in your own life when someone made fun of you for your morals. Has anyone ever dropped a relationship with you because you would not do something you knew was wrong?

## Tainted?

Whatever life was like for Lot's wife in Sodom, her family's actions suggest that each member might have been tainted by the evil around them. Consider the following from our text: the family's reluctance to obey the two angels, Lot's offer of his daughters to the mob, Lot's desire to escape to another city instead of to the hills as the angels directed, the disobedience of Lot's wife, the subsequent drunkenness of Lot, and the incestuous relationship the daughters proposed and carried out. What might each action indicate about the influence of wicked city inhabitants on the moral character of Lot's family?

## Leaving Sodom

Note verses 16 through 26. The messengers of God (angels) had urged the family to leave the city, but Lot and his family lingered through the night. At dawn, these men finally seized the reluctant family by the hands and led them out of the city. They gave strict instructions to them: "Don't look back and don't stop anywhere until you get to the hills." Clear and concise. Go. Don't look back. Don't stop. The wrath of God was coming on the city, and it was imperative that the family escape to the hills *without looking back*. Otherwise, they could not be saved.

After granting Lot's request to go to a town nearby instead of to the hills, the men repeated, "Escape quickly!" And they did. The sun had fully risen as the family reached the little city of Zoar with Lot's wife lagging behind. Then chaos began for Sodom, and Lot's wife, in blatant disobedience to the message from God, looked back.

God's instructions had been clear. "Don't look back!" She chose to disobey and the result was devastating. Her disobedience brought sudden death, and her family was left without a wife and mother. Do you think the family's later incidents of drunkenness and incest would have occurred if she had obeyed God and then had been present with them? Of course, we do not know, but we do know she would have been alive as wife and mother.

## "Sticky" Eyes

When I read this account, silent words on a page, I find it easy to condemn Lot's wife for looking backward after being told not to. But ... if I am that woman and the burning city is my home, I confess the temptation to look would have been great. Would you also have yearned to see what was happening to your former home and to your friends and neighbors?

Whether we would have acted on that urge might depend on whether our hearts are tied to earth or to heaven. Whether our focus is on the here and now or on the treasures that are in God. Whether, spiritually, we are all in with God or not.

If Lot's wife had been all in, then she would have been seeking to obey God's every command. She would have believed without a doubt that God would destroy Sodom and

Gomorrah but save her life. She also would have believed, in her heart of hearts, that whatever was ahead was in the hands of the merciful and loving God. And because it was, she and her family would be cared for by Him through any circumstance.

Unfortunately, Lot's wife had "sticky" eyes. She could not keep her eyes from sticking to the things that were behind. Material things from her old life. Her home in an evil city. Centuries later King David would plead with God, "Turn my eyes from looking at worthless things; and give me life in your ways" (Ps 119:37). Lot's wife could have had life in God's ways, but she chose to look back at worthless things and lost her life.

## What Can I Learn from
## The Disobedient Woman?

About obedience? (See also 1 Sam 15:22; Rom 6:16)

About "looking back"? (See also 2 Pet 2:20–22; Luke 9:62)

\* \* \*

### To Think About

Can you think of reasons Lot moved from Zoar, the city he requested, to the hills? Why would he have been afraid (v 30)?

Is there a circumstance or a relationship from your past keeping you from moving forward? How has that affected you spiritually and emotionally? If so, what steps can you take to "unstick" your eyes?

Is there a command by God that you are having difficulty obeying, i.e., sexual purity, forgiving another, honoring parents, submitting, etc.? If so, what is your specific plan for growing spiritually in that area? Will you commit to writing it down on paper, or putting it in your phone notes, and checking your progress periodically?

# Chapter 3

## *The Conniving Woman*

Scripture Text: Genesis 39:1–23

*She winked at the brightly made-up face staring back at her from the water at the bottom of the deep bowl. Turning her head slightly and widening her eyes, she murmured, "Maybe a little more kohl." She knew that the darkly defined eyes of an Egyptian woman would surely be alluring to a plain and simple but handsome Hebrew slave boy. "Boy, hah!" she exclaimed aloud.*

*"Did you say something, madam?" asked the attendant holding ready an outer garment for her mistress. Without replying, the mistress waved her hand in dismissal. "Leave me now," she commanded as she slipped the garment over her head. The attendant bowed and silently left the room.*

*As she picked up a piece of kohl from the table, her thoughts immediately returned to the slave boy. "He's no boy!" she cried as she swiped the dark substance emphatically over her eyelids and under each eye. "In fact," she thought, "Joseph seems to be about my age. Well, at least he's much older than I was when I married twelve years ago." That thought brought an image of her pudgy husband, Potiphar, whose only expressed interest, besides his job, seemed to be related to food. "When will my dinner be served?!" he usually bellowed on entering the house. What a contrast to the polite and deferential slave, Joseph, whose broad shoulders and well-defined muscles she had definitely noticed.*

*"That old Potiphar looks like a toad beside Joseph!" she acknowledged, throwing off the loose outer garment and rummaging through her clothes for something a little more figure-defining. Although Joseph did not raise his eyes when she spoke to him, she knew how to get him to do more than bow to her. "Aha!" she crowed, holding up a tunic that she thought showed off her beauty. "This is more like it!"*

*Slipping the garment over her head and belting it tightly so that every curve was defined, she smiled as she plotted how she could make sure he saw her. No man could surely resist such a beautiful woman as she! She would make sure that Joseph did not.*

\* \* \*

## Why?

Was Potiphar's wife in an unhappy marriage? Was she bored? Was she feeling unattractive? Was she captivated by Joseph's foreign-ness? Did she feel that she could command anything of a slave? Or was she practicing her "conquest" skills? We can only speculate, for her reasons for such an intense pursuit are unknown.

Whatever her motivations, Potiphar's wife displayed cunning and conniving behavior in this account. She saw something she wanted, and she determined to get it. Her objective, which she must have thought would be simple to achieve, was sexual relations with a handsome slave who had been purchased by her own husband. But there was something she did not know. She had not reckoned on the slave being a man of godly character.

## Background

A few years prior to this account (see Gen 37), the teen-aged Joseph had been wrenched from his comfortable home in Hebron where he was the favorite, and perhaps pampered, son of his father Jacob. His jealous brothers sold him to a band of Ishmaelites (*his distant relatives through great-grandfather Abraham*) who then traveled to Egypt. They eventually sold him as a slave to Potiphar, the captain of Pharaoh's guard.

As captain of Pharaoh's guard, Potiphar perhaps had wealth and a position that allowed him to own slaves to tend his large household while he served Pharaoh. The captain learned quickly that Joseph was a valuable and trustworthy worker who accepted responsibility and did his tasks well.

Through the ensuing years, Potiphar heaped more and more responsibility on Joseph's shoulders until he was overseeing all of Potiphar's considerable possessions. A large house surrounded by its many acres and the material possessions that such a man might have owned were in Joseph's complete care. From Joseph's later words, it seems that there must have been mutual trust and respect in this relationship of owner and slave.

## The Pursuit

Just when it seemed things were going well for Joseph, Satan, always active, seized the opportunity to interfere by using the wife of Joseph's owner. Joseph had matured during his years in Egypt and had grown from a teenager to a man. He is described in this account as handsome and well-built. The Bible states that Potiphar's wife "cast her eyes upon him" (v7). What does that phrase suggest to you?

Potiphar's wife was brash and relentless. She brazenly

asked Joseph to have sexual relations with her. Joseph's calm but firm refusal to her first advance noted her husband's great trust in him. Just as firmly, he went directly to the heart of the matter. He asked her how he could be so wicked and sin against God by betraying her husband's trust.

None of that made a difference to her. She pursued Joseph daily. She had found somebody she wanted, and she intended to have him.

## Satan's Opportunity

Satan, ever alert, went to work for a woman bent on doing wrong. He would give her the perfect opportunity. One day when Joseph entered the house to work, none of the other men were there. There was only his master's wife. She may have arranged for the men to have tasks elsewhere, but even if she did not, she certainly recognized this prime opportunity. She clutched at Joseph's tunic and pleaded with him. This time Joseph did not even take the time to risk an answer. He recognized evil for what it was and fled from it so swiftly that he left his garment in her hands.

## From Pursuit to Vengeance

Witnessing that quick flight, Potiphar's wife had a whiplash change of emotions. This woman's physical desire for a handsome young slave overturned in a split second to vengeance toward this same man who had so decidedly rejected her advances. She plotted her next steps.

Does her swift turn from relentless pursuit to vengeful accusation surprise you? In light of her earlier actions, what do you think was the reason Potiphar's wife sought so quickly to accuse Joseph falsely? Remember, no one witnessed what had occurred. No one would tell her husband. No one would accuse her.

Read carefully her explanations to the men of the household and then to Potiphar himself. Can you count the lies she told? Why do you think she played the "race card" when she mentioned "this Hebrew"? Notice how many times her husband's ethnicity (and likely hers) was mentioned in verses 1 through 5. When she told her story, who did she indicate was ultimately to blame?

Readers of this account know the actions that followed her accusations. Potiphar had Joseph thrown into prison after his wife's false disclosure. This action suggests a lesser punishment for such a transgression.[1] As one writer has noted, the choice of prison seems to indicate "Potiphar's understanding of the affair between Joseph and his wife. Rather than being executed for rape (as dictated in, for instance, the Middle Assyrian law), Joseph was put into a royal prison holding political prisoners."[2]

That means that Potiphar put Joseph into "the king's prison, of which, in his capacity as chief of the body-guard, he was the superintendent".[3] What do you think about Potiphar confining Joseph in the same prison that he oversaw (see v 20)?

## God's Providence

As always, God's providence was alive and working, even in prison. God used the result of the devious schemes of Potiphar's wife (Joseph being imprisoned) to provide the slave with another opportunity to hone the leadership skills he had been developing in Potiphar's house.

Now, in addition to what he had already learned about managing a large estate, Joseph would learn how to lead, care for, and manage a population in a difficult circumstance.

He was not in prison long until he had won the trust and favor of the keeper of the prison who soon put Joseph in charge of all the prisoners. Verse 22 of our text notes that "whatever was done there, he was the one who did it." The Lord was with Joseph in prison, just as He was with him as a slave in Potiphar's house, and just as He continued to be throughout Joseph's life.

## Concluding Thoughts

Potiphar's wife is not mentioned again in the scriptures. If she was still living, how do you think she felt about Joseph becoming, in just a few short years, second in command to Pharaoh? How might that have impacted her life? Did she ever experience remorse for her actions? We do not know the answers to those questions. We can only surmise that she perhaps continued acting upon her emotions of the moment and transgressing the stated or understood boundaries of others.

Potiphar's wife was a woman without sexual or moral boundaries. She evidently had no scruples about getting what she wanted, even as she trampled over the boundaries of another. Although this account focuses on the firm faith and commitment of Joseph, there are lessons that can be learned by taking a closer look at the married woman who was plotting his ruin.

## What Can I Learn from
## The Conniving Woman?

## Respect for Boundaries

*The boundary of God's relationship with another person.*

This account gives a picture of a woman who disregarded Joseph's declaration of his responsibility toward God. "How can I do this great wickedness and sin against God?" he asked her. She disrespected the very personal love and trust between Joseph and God.

*The boundary of marriage.*

Potiphar's wife displayed no regard for the boundary of her own marriage. A marriage boundary firmly encloses commitment, love, trust, and sexual exclusiveness between a husband and wife only. She was willing to violate her commitment and responsibility to her husband by trampling that boundary and was expecting Joseph to have no regard for the same boundary. After reading Genesis 2:24; Matthew 19:5-6; and Ephesians 5:31-33, how would you describe the boundaries God gave to marriage?

*Personal moral boundaries.*

Potiphar's wife disregarded Joseph's moral boundaries which he clearly delineated. He would not betray the trust of another, he would not engage in wicked behavior, and he would not sin against God. He had a need to be morally pure before his God. He said "no" to her numerous times. She ignored his firm refusals.

*Boundaries existing between someone in a dominant position and one in a lesser position.*

Potiphar's wife sexually harassed Joseph for an extended period. This was particularly egregious behavior because she was in the position of owner and he was her slave. Today, we understand this dynamic in the roles of employer and employee, teacher and student, doctor and patient, coach and athlete, or in any relationship where there is a real or perceived disparity in position.

* * *

## To Think About

Think about instances in which your own boundaries, in any area of life, have been ignored or disrespected. What emotions did you have when that happened?

What are specific ways that you can ensure that your moral boundaries are in place and displayed or known to others?

If you are married, what are specific ways you can be sure that you respect your marriage boundaries? In what ways can you display clear marriage boundaries for others to see? What can you do if someone trespasses those boundaries?

# Chapter 4

## *The Resolute Young Woman*

### Scripture Text: Judges 11

*She remembers her cousin's happy wedding celebration with all the colorful clothing, the joyous laughter of the guests and the way the groom's friends teased him. When she had asked her mother that night whether she would ever have such a ceremony, her mother had answered, "Of course, little one. Someday your father will select just the right person for you to marry and we will have a great wedding feast for you." Mother had cupped her daughter's face in her hands and bent to look her square in the eyes. "But that is a few years away, and we will enjoy the rest of the years we have with you."*

*She remembers how she had felt safe in her mother's hands then and how trusting she was that her father would find just the right man for her. After all, she had always known she was loved without reservation and that father would do anything he could for her. How long ago that talk with Mother seems now! And how distraught her father is now!*

*Today her heart is heavy as she selects necessary items for the next two months. For a moment sorrow threatens to overwhelm her, but she is determined not to give in to it. She is going to treat this time away as a mourning for what will never be but also as a celebration with friends.*

*She has carefully selected the other girls who will attend her as if she were selecting them for the wedding that will never happen. They will weep and mourn together, but they will also enjoy being together. She will especially enjoy their chatter and their many late-night talks. She must remember to display her happiness for their marriages that will take place in the next year or so. Some are betrothed already. Above all, she is resolved to enjoy their company, for when she returns, everything changes.*

* * *

## Life's Direction

Have you ever witnessed the direction of an entire life changed because of words spoken without complete fore-thought? The entire life of the young woman of Israel in our lesson text was changed because of a vow made to the Lord by her father Jephthah.

The fulfillment of Jephthah's vow ensured that his family tree would have no branches. His daughter, his only child, would never marry or bear children. There would be no grandson who might carry his name or be a mighty warrior like his grandfather. There would be no granddaughter who would bear children to be his descendants. His hasty vow to God meant the end of the family line for Jephthah, and it meant that his daughter's life, as she knew it, ceased.

## Background

Israel was in a mess. They had a great army of Ammonites ready to attack them, but they had no warrior to lead an army for them. The only one they knew was Jephthah, labeled "a mighty warrior" in our scripture text. But Jephthah had been driven out of the land by his half-brothers, who did not want to share an inheritance with him. After all, they must have thought, they were legitimate sons of their mother and father while Jephthah's mother had been a prostitute.

What a dilemma for the elders of the land! They would have to persuade this exiled man, who surely bore some animosity toward them, to swallow his pride and lead their army in pursuit of their enemy.

Perhaps Jephthah's fighting spirit began to be honed when he lived among his half-brothers who clearly rejected him and any claim he had to his father's legacy. But his warrior skills were surely polished by his time in exile in the land of Tob. He obviously had leadership skills because he began to attract a small army of "worthless" men, as they are described in our text. The term "worthless" is translated in other versions as "scoundrels" (NIV) and "vain" (KJV). Clarke's Commentary notes that the men were not necessarily criminals but could be "poor persons without property, and without employment".[1] They might have been much like the group of men who first gathered around David before he was king. David's group of men protected the villages around them in exchange for necessities.

Because of succeeding events, the people of Israel obviously knew about the success of Jephthah's motley group. When the elders of Israel approached Jephthah, they offered to him leadership of the entire Israelite army in Gilead so that they could fight their enemies. But Jephthah was not easy to persuade. He reminded them that they had despised him and thrown him out of the land. Then he asked them for the reason they had now come begging him to help in their distress.

The elders did not deny Jephthah's assessment of their behavior but only repeated their request, emphasizing this time that he would be the leader of *all* the inhabitants in Gilead. Jephthah offered a stipulation to their offer. He would be leader *if* God let him be victorious in the battle. The elders of Israel agreed.

Jephthah's first action as leader of the army was to question the enemy. He asked the Ammonites about the reason for the fight they wanted. They answered with a claim that Israel had taken over their land when they came out of Egypt some 300 years before.

Jephthah set them straight by giving them a history lesson. He detailed the truth that Israel had only asked to pass through their lands, but the Ammonites had refused. He emphasized that it was God, not the Israelites that had dispossessed the people of their land. He then asked God, the Judge, to decide between the people of Ammon and the people of Israel. The Ammonite king refused to listen. Jephthah and his army began then to move toward the enemy.

## Jephthah's Vow

With the Spirit of the Lord upon him, Jephthah moved his army from Tob, passing through the lands of Gilead and Manasseh. He left the city of Mizpah to head toward the battle with the Ammonites. Along the way, Jephthah made a vow to God.

Perhaps he wanted to encourage the army. Or maybe he was trying to set an example of leadership by offering something of his to the Lord. His vow seemed to be motivated by a love for God and a willingness to give, but the vow was not well-reasoned. One writer notes that "there is no indication that God approved of Jephthah's vow."[2] Jephthah vowed to God that if He would give the enemy into his hands, he would give to the Lord the first thing that came out of his house when he returned from battle.

Perhaps when Jephthah had returned from previous raids a servant had exited the doors of his house first to greet the returning warrior. Or perhaps another family member had come out of the doors. Whatever or whoever greeted him first had certainly not been his daughter. Otherwise, he never would have made the vow.

## Jephthah's Daughter

The great warrior's daughter, whose name is not given in the scriptures, was Jephthah's only child. We can only imagine the kind of life an only child, and evidently well-loved daughter, lived in a household such as Jephthah's. The Scriptures tell us nothing about Jephthah's wife, but we can assume that both mother and father doted on their only child. She would have been lovingly cared for by both parents and servants alike.

Both father and mother must have had dreams for this well-loved child's future. Perhaps they dreamed of her marriage to a wealthy and loving husband. They surely must have anticipated and longed for the grandchildren that would fill up their empty house and bring them great joy. They could not know that their dreams would be so far from the coming reality.

## Jephthah's Return

The daughter obviously loved and was proud of her father, the mighty warrior. She must have had difficulty waiting until the conquering hero came home from battle. Word had already reached the household that the war was over and the Israelites were the conquerors. Jephthah and his men were on their way home. Perhaps runners brought word of the army's progress as they moved closer to Mizpah.

The day of arrival finally came. The men were just outside

their home city. Eagerly anticipating their arrival, the daughter had tambourines ready for a grand celebration.

When the men arrived, this well-loved daughter was excited. There would be no more war. Her father would now be home. She danced out the door to greet him with tambourines jangling, joyously celebrating her father's great victory over the Ammonites.

She must have been surprised at her father's anguished reaction. The dance stopped and the tambourines stilled. Jephthah did not return her celebratory greeting. Instead, he responded with a symbol of great grief. He tore his clothes.

His first words to her were filled with plaintive and mournful chiding for bringing such trouble on him. He then told her that he had made a vow to the Lord that he could not take back.

Evidently understanding that his vow had something to do with her, her response was immediate and calm. She told her father that whatever his vow meant for her, he must fulfill it.

## The Daughter's Request

After learning what the vow entailed, Jephthah's daughter asked that she be allowed to go away for a period of two months. Knowing that she would never marry or bear children, she wanted to go to the mountains with her girlfriends to "bewail her virginity." Jephthah granted her request.

The daughter and her companions traveled to the mountains for the allotted time and "wept for her virginity" as the text indicates. Upon her return, Jephthah fulfilled his vow.

## Controversy About the Vow

Let's revisit the vow in Judges 11:30–31 and note exactly what Jephthah promised. "If you will give the Ammonites into my hand, then whatever comes out from the doors of my house to meet me when I return in peace from the Ammonites shall be the Lord's, and I will offer it up for a burnt offering."

This vow has created several questions for readers. One of those questions is this: Would Jephthah really keep his vow if it involved such an unintended sacrifice? God had given specific instructions about vows in the law he gave. What God said as recorded in Numbers 30:1–2 and Deuteronomy 23:21–23 specifies that a person who has made a vow to the Lord should keep it.

A second question is this: How did God feel about human sacrifice? The sacrifice of humans was associated with the pagan religions in areas surrounding God's children, and He said, in no uncertain terms, that it was an abomination to Him. Read Leviticus 18:21; 20:1–5; Deuteronomy 12:31; 18:10–13 for His instructions about this horrific practice.

A third question is the most pressing and controversial of all: Did Jephthah keep his vow by sacrificing his daughter as a burnt offering? Verse 39 of our text stated that when the daughter returned, Jephthah "did with her according to his vow that he had made." That verse seemed to indicate the answer to the third question should be "yes." But ... .

## Possible Explanation

Our understanding of the vow could actually hang on the translation of a small Hebrew conjunction in the text passage. Let's review the vow one more time. Jephthah stated that whatever came out the doors of his house first should be the Lord's *and* he would sacrifice it on the altar.

The Hebrew word for *and* in that text is *vau*, according to Jackson and Wood, used also in 1 Chronicles 21:11–12 and Exodus 21:15 where it is translated *or*.[3] The translation of this Hebrew word in our text passage as *or* instead of *and*, "flows better with the context and the rest of scripture," as Merrill notes.[4] Jephthah's vow would then be that whatever came out the doors of his house would be the Lord's, *or* he would offer it up for a burnt offering. Using the conjunction *or* means if what came out of the doors was not suitable for a burnt offering, then it would be sacrificed in dedication to the Lord.

This translation of scripture seems to offer a clearer reason for the two-month journey to the mountains requested by the daughter. Jephthah's daughter did not want to bewail her death, but her virginity. She would remain a virgin all of her life.

In addition, this translation makes clearer a seemingly random statement, "she knew no man" (v 39), after she had returned home and after the fulfillment of the vow. Otherwise, this sentence is, in the words of one writer, "a completely superfluous and callous remark if she had been put to death."[5]

The fact that she would never bear children, generally considered a woman's main purpose in Old Testament times, changed the entire direction of this daughter's life. God's instruction to "be fruitful and multiply" would not apply to her as a woman whose sole purpose from that point forward would be to serve God and Him alone.

## Concluding Thoughts

If we understand the vow in this manner, we also understand the depth of Jephthah's grief in a different way. His daughter will live, not die, but she will never marry and have children. There will be no lavish wedding celebration. There will be no son-in-law nor grandchildren. There will be no perpetuation of Jephthah's name. He will have no descendants. Heartbreaking for such a strong warrior leader.

While this was surely heartbreaking to both Jephthah and

his daughter, we must admire the resolve of this young woman. Our lesson text gives no indication that she ever faltered. While her father was in grief about his vow when he saw her, she did not hesitate. As she pointed out, he must carry out the vow. At the end of the two-month mourning period, she resolutely returned to her father so that he could fulfill the vow he had made to God.

## What Can I Learn from
## The Resolute Young Woman

About joy in the battles God has won for you? (1 Sam 17:47; 2 Chron 20:15)

About being serious about and obedient to commandments of God? (1 John 5:3; Jer 7:23–24)

About being subject to God even when your fate has been determined by another? (Jas 4:10)

*  *  *

### To Think About

When have you been affected negatively because of something someone else said or did?

Has your family celebrated any victories that God has given?

Have you ever made a vow or promise to God that you have not kept? What was the result? If so, what plan will you make to remember to follow through with the promise?

# Chapter 5

## *The Otherworldly Woman*

**Scripture Text: 1 Samuel 28:3–25**

*"What is that?" She jerked her head toward the scratch of gravel in the night. "Footsteps?" Her muscles tensed. A flutter of fear made her stomach uneasy. No one else would have heard the almost silent steps of those who climbed stealthily over small rocks embedded at strategic points in the pathway. But then she was not just anyone. The law forbidding the dark arts she had long practiced and the exile of her fellow practitioners had made her alert to any changes in the environment. The threat of possible death honed her senses to a needle-sharp awareness.*

*She peered around the doorway into the starless night. "Who's there?" she whispered, beginning to discern the faint outlines of three men. A voice belonging to the tall shadowed figure in front called softly, "Do not fear! It is just a man who requests a favor from you."*

*"Stop there, please!" she demanded. A few seconds passed. "What favor?" she asked warily but more softly.*

*His reply increased her anxiety. "I want you to bring up from the dead whoever I mention to you," he said quietly.*

*She shrank against the door frame. "Do you not know that the king has outlawed such things and has put away those who practice them?" she cried. "You have been sent as a trap for me. To grant your wish would be my death!"*

*Invoking the name of God, the man stepped closer and swore she would receive no punishment. She thought quickly. She needed the money he would pay. Since the edict had been issued, many no longer came to ask her help, and those few who sneaked to her doorway paid only what they wished, knowing that she dared not demand more without consequences.*

*These men standing outside her door tonight were strangers but ... the tall one had sworn to her safety by God himself. Her decision made, she asked, "Who do you want me to bring up for you?"*

*His answer did nothing to quiet her fears.*

\* \* \*

## Fear and Desperation

King Saul was in deep trouble. The Israelites, under Saul, were preparing for battle with the Philistines, and, seeing the size of the Philistine army, Saul was afraid. In fact, he was terrified.

The king had asked God about the outcome of the battle. But because of Saul's disobedience with actions that indicated an ungodly heart, God did not answer him. (See 1 Sam 15 for an account of Saul's disobedience).

Saul's intense fear turned to desperation, and desperate people often do desperate things. The prophet Samuel had always helped Saul before. Saul reasoned that if Samuel were only here, he could tell Saul what he should do. But there was only one problem. Samuel was dead.

A desperate thought must have come to Saul in his deep fear. "I know what I will do! I will have Samuel brought back from the dead! Then he can tell me what to do!" Now that is a desperate thought!

Saul determined to find someone who could do that for him. But there was another problem with that idea. Saul, in line with the law God gave to Moses for the Israelites (see Lev 19:31; 20:6, 27; Deut 18:9–14) had put out of the land all those who were alleged to divine the future and to traffic with dead spirits.

## The Anti-Divine Search

Just so this situation is clear: King Saul wants to find a person who can help divine the future, but that will be difficult because he himself has expelled from the kingdom all those who practice such things. The king wants to break the law of God and the law he has espoused in his role as king. This act alone shows the depth of his despair.

Saul made the decision, anyway. He directed his servants to seek out a medium of whom he could inquire. This single action, seeking an answer for God's people from someone who practices the pagan dark arts, shows how far Saul had distanced himself from God. As one writer noted, Saul was "seeking the Divine through the anti-Divine."[1]

Because of Saul's edict regarding mediums and diviners, there were, supposedly, not any in the land. But somehow the servants knew just where to find one. By the law, this medium that servants knew about should have been dead, stoned by the people for her pagan practices in Israel, but there she was living in the shadows in Endor.

## The Medium

In an attempt not to be seen, Saul put on a disguise. Then he crept to the medium's house at night with two of his men.

The medium's reaction when Saul told her his request to bring someone back from the dead is certainly ironic. She told the king, unrecognized by her, that the king had forbidden such practices. As if he didn't know!

The medium had no powers except what God allowed her to have. We do not know why God allowed Samuel to come back from the dead. The text just indicates that he appeared when the medium called. And that medium seemed to be the one most surprised by his appearance. She suddenly cried out when she saw him, knowing she had been deceived. How do you think she knew that the dead person she saw was Samuel and that the man standing with her was Saul, the king?

There is no indication that Saul ever saw Samuel as he came back from the dead because the king asked the medium to describe what she saw. When she described the spirit she saw, noting the robe, Saul knew it was Samuel (see also 15:27). He immediately knelt and bowed to pay homage to that great prophet.

Samuel said nothing to calm Saul's fears. Instead, he reminded Saul that disobedience had caused Saul's current trouble, and, furthermore, Saul and his sons would be killed in battle the following day. Upon that news, Saul fell prone to the ground, completely without strength. Interestingly and, one might think, out of character, the medium had compassion on Saul and provided food for him and his men.

## What Can I Learn from
## The Otherworldly Woman?

## About Divination

Although this biblical account took place more than 3,000 years ago, divination has remained even into our modern times. Today, we still have psychics, fortunetellers, astrologers, and those who purport to tell the future through reading tea leaves, palms, cards, crystals, or astrological signs.

A former White House Chief of Staff relates in his memoir that even the occupants of the White House during his time consulted a medium. He stated that every major decision the occupants made "was cleared in advance with a woman in San Francisco who drew up horoscopes to make certain that the planets were in a favorable alignment for the enterprise."[2]

Why would God call the practice of such things "abominable"? What is wrong with divination? In forming your answer, read the following passages: Leviticus 19:31 and 20:7, 8, 26, 27 and 1 Samuel 15:22, 23.

From the scriptures above, can you state here in one sentence the basic issue with divination?

## About Evil Practitioners

People who do evil things are seldom all evil. We frequently read statements by friends or family of those who have committed some heinous crime. The person often states "I am so surprised. He was such a nice neighbor. He looked after our dog when we were away." Or another says, "I can't believe this. Every time we met, she asked about my mother (father, sister, child)" or "He always gave money to anyone who needed it."

In the same manner, the medium at Endor was not all evil. She exhibited compassion as she saw the king's complete collapse following Samuel's pronouncement to him. Observing that Saul needed food, she set about to kill and cook a fattened calf and bake bread. The hours that must have taken perhaps allowed Saul and his men to rest. Surely, the food was well received and gave them strength to face what they must. And what they must face was a devastating battle and death for the king and perhaps for the men who accompanied him to the medium.

The kind and caring acts of those who are engaged in activities that are abhorrent to God often sway those of us who are trying to live for Him. Because those people are kind and caring in some things, we may begin to approve all things they do.

While the medium at Endor was compassionate and caring toward Saul, she was still involved in abominable practices. A few kind deeds do not negate things done in rebellion to God. Our task as Christians is to discern rebellious practices, resist their pull on us, and help to stop them in ourselves and in others if possible. If stopping them is not possible, we definitely must not approve the practices, or, to use a modern term, "embrace" them.

## Definitions

Divination: "The practice of attempting to foretell future events or discover hidden knowledge by occult or supernatural means."[3]

Necromancer: One who "uses witchcraft or sorcery, especially to reanimate dead people or to foretell the future by communicating with them."[4]

Medium: "A person through whom communications are thought to be sent to the living from spirits of the dead."[5]

# Chapter 6

## The Dramatic Woman

Scripture Text: 2 Samuel 14:1–20

*She fingered through the clothes in the ancient wardrobe before picking up the dark mourning robe. As she clutched it close, the coarse fibers reminded her of the days her mother and father were laid in the tomb with their ancestors. She felt a fresh stab of grief as she held it in front of her, looking carefully for any loose threads or tears in the fabric. Placing the robe on the bed covering, she began to look for the head covering that went with it.*

*"Ah!" she exclaimed, picking up the rectangle of material. "This should be just right!" Her grief quickly forgotten, she smiled as she pictured the scene. She would be in her mourning clothes telling a sorrowful tale with weeping and begging in front of the great King David on his throne.*

*She knew he would believe her for, after all, had she not been performing since she was a small child? She chuckled remembering her friends gathering around as she entertained them with tall tales and mimicry. And how many times had her mother told her to stop all the drama and do what she had asked her to do? Too many times to count!*

*As her hands brushed across the rough material of the robe and headpiece, she remembered her visit with Joab. A "wise" woman he had called her. She knew that her mind had grown strong through the years with keen insight into situations and problem. Those were gifts from God, and she longed to use them for Him. Joab presented her with a perfect opportunity.*

*That and her natural flair for dramatic behavior could help resolve the dilemma that had the nation holding its collective breath. King David was mourning for Absalom whom he had expelled from the land. "For a good reason!" she thought as she remembered the killing of Amnon. But then she thought about the detestable crime the murdered Amnon had committed against Absalom's sister, his own half-sister, and her heart softened. What a dilemma for King David!*

*She shook her head as if shaking out the thoughts. For now, she must get to the task. That was going to take a great deal of time. The words needed to be "just right" and she must say them in a most convincing manner. Joab had given her the basic outline of what was needed, but he had told it to her in flat words. She knew that to get and keep the king's attention, her approach needed to be convincing and flawless. He needed to believe her as a grieving widow.*

*She also knew he would comment and perhaps ask questions. She must anticipate those questions and be ready with believable answers. But those answers needed to be stated in the correct way for this astute king and also couched in a manner that he would appreciate.*

*A tale, but believable. A request, but actually a telling. A dramatic performance, but for the good of the kingdom.*

\* \* \*

## Dramatic Women

You know the type. Women with a flair. Self-assured, perhaps with a little sparkle and dazzle, such women command attention and sometimes ... indulgence. If the woman also has wisdom in her speech, she can indeed be a powerful force.

The woman of Tekoa seemed to be such a woman. Known as a wise woman, she was intelligent. Perhaps she had a lot of people knowledge and common sense. That is, she had learned through observation and trial how people commonly act during common circumstances and could gauge common reactions to various stimuli. She obviously had learned what life choices brought about good things for herself and others and which ones did not. All of these observations and innate understandings helped her to act wisely and to help others do the same.

For this task, however, other skills would be needed also. Joab was asking her to play a role in solving a problem. A dramatic role that could convince a king. The great King David was suffering and indecisive and something needed to be done. The woman's role was to become a grieving widow, convincing enough to move the king toward a decision. One that would get the king himself and his kingdom off high center.

## The Backstory (2 Samuel 13)

King David had numerous sons, but two of his sons (by different women) had been engaged in a silent war which ended in the death of one. Amnon, the oldest of David's sons and therefore heir to the throne, lusted after the beautiful Tamar, the full sister of David's second heir, Absalom.\*  Although Tamar was his half-sister, Amnon took advantage of a scheme devised by his crafty cousin Jonadab and raped Tamar when she came to care for him during a feigned illness. Are you already thinking this was some messed-up family? Read on.

Afterward, Absalom soothed his sister and suggested she "not take this to heart" (2 Sam 13:20). In other words, she should just forget about it. That must have sounded heartless to a royal young woman who had been so humiliated and disgraced, as it would to any young woman.

King David, Tamar's father, upon hearing about the incident "was furious" (v 21) but did nothing to the rapist, his own son. Absalom, however, was silently plotting revenge. After two years had passed, he devised a scheme to lure Amnon to his home along with all the other brothers for a feast during sheepshearing. At the feast, Absalom seized the opportunity and instructed his servants to kill Amnon. Then Absalom fled the country.

The great King David was an intentional leader of his kingdom and is described as a man after God's own heart. His fathering skills, however, were definitely less than admirable. He seemed to be indulgent (see 1 Kgs 1:5–6 about another son) and certainly was not tuned in to the actual character of his sons.

Note the lack of reactions: When Amnon had begged his father to let Tamar come to his house to make food for him during his faked illness, David expressed no suspicion of his motives. When Absalom specifically requested of the king that Amnon go with the other brothers to the feast at Absalom's house, David asked the reason, but then gave in when Absalom pressed him. When Absalom fled after killing Amnon, the likely heir, at the feast, the scriptures note that the king "mourned for his son day after day" and that the "spirit of the king longed to go out to Absalom," yet he did nothing (2 Sam 13:37, 39).

David mourned for his first son, a schemer and a rapist, and perhaps also for his other son, the conniver, plotter and murderer of David's firstborn. Quite a family!

## A Quandary

After he killed Amnon, Absalom fled to Geshur, where his maternal grandfather ruled as king (2 Sam 3:3). At the time of our reading, Absalom had sought refuge and lived for three years among his mother's relatives. David had grown older. The one in line to inherit his kingdom was in self-exile in another land.

Joab, the fierce and loyal leader of David's troops and his right-hand man began to think this problem needed to be solved. He saw David longing for his absent son. He noted the indecision. He decided something must be done, but the king was the only one who could recall Absalom. And the king was in a quandary.

Absalom had committed murder, prohibited by the sixth commandment. The law was plain about what needed to be done (Lev 24:17; Num 35:30–34). David was a follower of the law. But David did not go after his son. Absalom had been away for three years by the time this account takes place. David's need for vengeance had weakened. Amnon was dead, and David was "comforted" about him (v 39).

Joab took matters into his own hand and sought someone that he thought could help. He summoned a wise woman from Tekoa and told her what he needed her to do. There was no hesitation on her part. She took him seriously and planned how she would get an audience with the king.

## Before the King

The woman put on quite a performance. She was so convincing she could have been a nominee for an acting award. And what a speech! A compelling story, filled with flattery and colorful metaphors, told by a poor widow who begged for the life of her only surviving son. And David never suspected all of it was "fake news."

Wearing her mourning clothes, she told the king she was a widow. She and her husband had two sons. While the sons were in the field, they quarreled and because there was no one there to intervene, one son killed the other. The whole family was now asking that the murder be avenged. They were calling for the death of the other son, and she begged the king to protect that son, who was the only heir to the family name and possessions. Note that this "fake" family calling for revenge was following the law that God Himself gave the nation for its own good (Deut 19:11–13).

David told her to go home, and he would give orders about her situation. But the woman only pressed harder. She pleaded with him to give specific orders right then that the blood avenger would not harm her son. She noted through a compelling metaphor that the "only coals" left to her would go out if her son was killed. The king softened. He even gave an oath by God's name that vengeance against her son would not be carried out.

Only then did she let the shoe drop. The real reason she was there. This had not been her son, but the king's treatment of his son that was actually the subject of her plea. She confronted him, much as Nathan the prophet had done about his sin with Bathsheba, by telling him he convicted himself by promising her son would live. If he promised that not a hair of her son's head would be harmed, why could not his own son receive the same treatment? The trap had sprung.

David understood immediately what had been happening in front of him. He could not pardon her son and not pardon his own. He also understood who was responsible for her performance for he asked if Joab was behind her plea. She replied truthfully.

She had done what she came for. The king saw his situation clearly through her parable. Now he must not go back on his word. He had told her in front of the entire court that her son would not be harmed. David had to arrange for Absalom to come home. He gave the order to Joab.

## The Truth of the Matter

The Scriptures have nothing more to say about the woman from Tekoa. Perhaps she went home, satisfied with her performance before the king. Later, when Absalom was welcomed back by his father, she may have felt good that she had a part in that.

But ... I wonder if she had a twinge of doubt as Absalom schemed against his father to gain the trust and hearts of men in the kingdom. And I wonder if stirrings of regret began when Absalom openly conspired against David to proclaim himself king while David was still alive. When Absalom assembled his troops and waged open warfare against his father, was she astonished that someone who had received that much grace could war against the grace-giver? And when Absalom died by the hand of the very one who had asked her to come before the king, did she fall on her knees and ask God to forgive her for the part she played?

## Concluding Thoughts

The truth of the matter is that the woman from Tekoa urged David to break a law that God had put in place so that his people would not be defiled. David had already violated one of God's laws when he did nothing to Amnon for the rape he committed (Lev 18:9 and Deut 22:28–29). David had then ignored another of God's laws. Those laws perhaps seem harsh to us in this modern age, but God was preparing His people to be different from any other nation. His people needed to cleanse their land of defilement.

We will never know, of course, what this particular woman in the shadows felt or thought about the outcome of her performance. We don't know if her moment of glory in standing before the king faded as Absalom's pride and arrogance came to full bloom. And we don't know if she fully realized that her dramatic performance, effective as it was, came to a bitter end for both father and son. When David cried out, "O my son Absalom, my son, my son Absalom! Would I had died instead of you, O Absalom, my son, my son!" (2 Sam 18:33) did it echo in her ears, and in her heart, as she realized what she had helped to bring about.

* 2 Samuel 3:2–4 and 5:14 list the names of David's sons who were born in Hebron and in Jerusalem. Note that Absalom is listed as the third son. David's second son, Chileab, whose mother was Abigail, is never mentioned in Scripture as a possible heir. Some scholars conjecture that he possibly died at an early age; thus, Absalom would be second in line as a successor.

## What Can I Learn from
## The Dramatic Woman?

About doing my best when I have a task? (See Eccl 9:10; Col 3:23–24)

About obedience to my leaders? (Rom 13:1–5; 1 Tim 5:17, 19; Heb 13:17)

\* \* \*

## To Think About

Have you ever been asked by a leader to complete a task by using a special ability of yours?

Have you ever been asked to use your ability to complete a task that you later regretted?

Specify the abilities (talents) God has given you and the ways He has helped you develop them. How have you used them to honor Him? If you haven't, what are some ways that you can begin to do so?

# Chapter 7

## *The Self-Sacrificing Woman*

### Scripture Text: 1 Kings 17:8–24

*Dust, filtering through the covering over her nose and mouth, swirled around her bent head. She coughed weakly and blinked her eyes repeatedly to clear them. Spying a thin stick lodged against the wall, she added it to the other one in her hand. The stick reminded her of her son's rail-thin arms and legs.*

*Quick tears helped to clear dust from her eyes. "Tears seem to be the only wet things here," she thought, glancing at the brittle grass and clumps of brown, leafless brush surrounding the city gates.*

*A picture flashed in memory. Her son, riding on strong shoulders, hands holding to his father's ears and squealing with laughter as they herded their few sheep toward the lush grass. With an overwhelming longing for the long-gone, but never forgotten, tall man with the same easy smile as her son, she murmured, "We'll be with you soon."*

*She thought back through the seasons since his death. While the years had brought heavy burdens, she and her son had cared for themselves with the sheep, a few vines and olive trees, a small garden and the kindness of neighbors and relatives. That is, they had until the gardens and fields died without rain, streams dried into rutted depres-*

*sions, and neighbors dared not share without starving their own children.*

*"So, today begins the end," she thought with resignation and a measure of relief. The incessant search for food would be over, and the fears that kept her awake through the night would be gone. She whispered, "My son must go before I do. I cannot bear to think he would die in fear and alone."*

*Those words brought more tears. "Enough of this!" she said forcefully as she straightened, determination replacing her tears.*

*Had she still been crying, she might have missed seeing a figure making his way through the arid landscape surrounding Zarephath. Tall and imposing, the man steadily strode toward the city gate.*

*"Poor stranger," she thought. "He will find scant relief here." Watching as he drew closer, she felt a prickling along her spine. There was something about him. Squinting in the harsh sun, she spied the mantle around his shoulders.*

\* \* \*

## Famine

Those of us reading this lesson live in developed countries in modern times. With fully stocked grocery stores and restaurants serving all types of food, we struggle to understand famine and starvation. If one of our regions has scarce rain and a bad crop season, we simply import food from another region or country with a full growing season. But in the days of this lesson, things were much different. Without rain for grain crops, and fruit trees, and vineyards, and grazing land, neither people nor animals could survive.

This biblical account takes place during the reign of King Ahab of Israel. And the drought was the king's fault!

Ahab had married Jezebel, whose father ruled over Sidon, a pagan area north of Israel. After their marriage, Ahab introduced and promoted among God's own people, the worship of Baal, a pagan god of weather and fertility. The Scriptures record that Ahab "did more to provoke the Lord, the God of Israel, to anger than did all the kings of Israel before him" (1 Kgs 16:33). God did not take the worship of idols lightly.

His punishment was that Israel would have no rain or dew until He decided to bring rain again. King Ahab needed to learn that everything, even rainfall, is under God's control. God's prophet Elijah revealed the news of the coming drought to Ahab.

## The Calling

Shortly afterward, God called Elijah to go to the town of Zarephath, a town in Sidon, the land belonging to Queen Jezebel's father. As God's prophet, Elijah had fought and would continue to fight against the idol worship among God's people for all the 22 years of Ahab's reign. Many of those battles were directly with Ahab and his evil wife.

I wonder what Elijah thought when God told him to journey to a pagan land ruled by the father of his enemy Jezebel. Whatever he thought or felt, he went when God called.

God planned for Elijah to show God's might and power to a Zarephath widow and her son who were facing starvation. Although outside Israel, Zarephath and its surrounding areas were also affected by the drought and suffered a devastating famine. In fact, the widow and her son were only a handful of flour and a little oil away from death by starvation.

The widow had already planned that she and her son would eat a small cake made from the two ingredients remaining in their house. After this meager meal, they would wait for death that would surely come not many days after.

There was no more food to be found, but she had not reckoned on the intervention of God in her life.

## Meeting God's Prophet

On the day of the proposed last meal, the widow was gathering sticks to build a small fire to cook her scant provisions. Suddenly, at the city gate she was face to face with God's intervention! There was Elijah, the prophet of God, outside the city about to meet a Gentile woman in that pagan land.

I wonder what the widow thought when, upon meeting her, the prophet requested a little water to drink. Water? Where was she going to find water, such a precious commodity in this parched land? Was there a small spring that was not yet dried and had a trickle of water? Had she saved a few tablespoons of water for the last meal? Was it her portion of that meal? Whatever she thought and felt about Elijah's request and wherever the source of water, she immediately took action to give him what he asked.

As she turned away to answer his request, the prophet had another request. He asked her to bring him a small piece of bread. At first glance the request seems almost cruel. A piece of bread! From a woman who was starving?

The widow answered the request for bread kindly and honestly. She had no bread, she told him. Only a handful of flour and a little oil in a jar. She then revealed her plan to bake a small cake for her and her son and wait for their deaths.

Notice Elijah's response. He acknowledged an understanding of her emotion when he spoke kindly to her. "Do not be afraid," he said. Then he told her to prepare a cake of bread for him first and bring it to him. After that she could make one for herself and her son.

I wonder what she thought of this command from a stranger who was looking at starvation in her face. Make a cake of bread for him first! Did she believe him when he told her not to be afraid?

Ah, but then he told her the good news. He revealed what was in store for her and from where it would come. She would have flour and oil until there was rain on the land, as commanded by the Lord, the God of Israel. This the great prophet said to a woman living in a pagan land who knew about Elijah's God but did not *know* Him.

What do you think were her thoughts as she went to prepare the cake for Elijah? Could she have been skeptical? Did she hesitate before giving this stranger a portion of her last remaining bit of food? Whatever her thoughts were, she obeyed the prophet who had spoken the words of God to her, and because of her obedience, her household had food until the rains came in the third year.

## Disaster Strikes

At some point the widow evidently provided an upper room for Elijah as he traveled so that he could do the work of God. Perhaps through their conversations she learned more about Elijah's God, and he grew to appreciate her and to have joy in her child.

After a time, however, disaster struck. Her child died. How devastated she must have been! She had seen her son saved from death by starvation only to have him stricken later by a deathly illness.

Her immediate response was to call the prophet. Obviously, she had witnessed God's provision of food for her household and was convinced that Elijah's God was powerful.

Thinking that her sins must have caused the death of her son, she accused Elijah of having something against her. Elijah's response was to grab the child and take him to Elijah's own bed upstairs.

He even challenged God. "Are you bringing calamity on the woman now by killing her son?" he cried.

Three times he stretched himself upon the son and cried to God to give the child life again. God heard Elijah and answered. The child lived. How elated the mother must have been as she saw her child coming down the steps in Elijah's arms!

## Her Growth in Faith

Her response at that moment indicates that she had finally realized God was real and that He spoke truth through Elijah. Notice the growth of her faith in verses 12, 18, and 24. She first spoke of the Lord as Elijah's God. Later, she recognized that Elijah was a man of God. But after seeing her son brought back to life, she acknowledged that God's word was true as it was spoken by Elijah.

God's providence had brought together this starving Gentile widow and Elijah. Through the relationship with God's prophet, this kindly woman witnessed the power and might of God. Through that miraculous power, she and her son were fed physically, and their lives were extended. But the spiritual food was the most important for, upon seeing her son brought from death to life, she was convinced that God's word, through Elijah, was true. A fortuitous meeting indeed!

### What Can I Learn from
### The Self-Sacrificing Woman?

About God calling us to do difficult, self-sacrificing things?
(See also Heb 12:3–4 and Jas 5:10–11)

About God's Word being for all? (See also Acts 10:34–35,
Col 3:11, Luke 4:25–26)

* * *

### To Think About

If you had been the widow, would you have granted Elijah's
requests? Why do you think God, through Elijah, requested
the water and the bread from a starving woman?

Have you ever had to do a hard thing in faith? What was the
outcome? What did you learn about God and about yourself
through that event?

Have you ever neglected to do something that was right but
was so hard you felt you couldn't do it? If so, was fear a
factor and what were you afraid of?

# Chapter 8

## The Hospitable Woman

### Scripture Text: 2 Kings 4:8–37; 8:1–6

*The donkey trotted quickly along the path, goaded often by the servant running alongside. The woman mounted on the animal gripped the leather strap in her hand and gathered her cloak more closely about her, her breathing ragged. Tears flowed freely, but she made no attempt to brush them away. She whispered quietly but intensely as she had done since mounting the donkey, the words indistinct to the servant.*

*Periodically she raised her head to stare at the mountain looming in the distance, as if her gaze could move it closer. She had exchanged no words with the servant since her early admonitions for speed, but her seriousness and concentration communicated to him the importance of this fifteen-mile journey.*

*When they reached the base of the mountain and began climbing, she gave no slack to the donkey as he stumbled slightly on the rocky incline but urged him on with her heels. The servant also prodded the animal, silently perceiving his mistress's need for speed. During the climb, she repeatedly glanced up in a desperate search for something or someone.*

*As the path began to level, she seemed to search more intently until finally she smiled slightly through the tears. Gehazi ran to meet her and asked about her welfare and that of her family. The servant at her side was surprised that his mistress did not break the stride of the donkey, but he was most astonished at the calmness of her answer to Gehazi's question, "All is well." He knew instinctively that all was not well with his mistress, but what was the reason?*

*She gazed piercingly into the distance without blinking until a mantled figure came into view. Her breathing quickened and the whispering was more fervent. As they drew closer, the servant watched as she suddenly dismounted and ran toward the man he knew as Elisha, whom he had often attended on visits to the master's house. The servant's eyes widened as his mistress fell to the ground before the prophet and grasped his feet as if she were chained to him. She was still mumbling and crying but seemed unable to speak aloud. His heart began to race. Things were definitely not well with his mistress.*

\* \* \*

## A Room of His Own

When the Shunammite woman invited the prophet Elisha to share a meal at her home, did she know they would have a years-long relationship? Did she have any idea that her hospitable offer to build a room just for Elisha would result in examples of God's love that would answer her two deepest desires? Perhaps not. At the time they met, she was just a notable woman of wealth who recognized a man of God and opened her home to him.

This woman's hospitality toward an itinerant prophet of God is commendable. When Elisha came to her town, she invited him to eat at her house. After that, any time Elisha was passing through Shunem, he visited her household and ate with her and her husband.

Not only did she provide food, but she suggested to her husband that they build a room on the flat roof of their house and put a few essential furnishings in it so that Elisha could use it as he traveled through Shunem. They did just that, and the room was put to use for Elisha and his servant Gehazi.

## A Deepest Desire Fulfilled

On one such occasion Elisha was resting in the room. Perhaps he looked around and remembered the kindness and thoughtfulness of the one who had prepared such a guestroom for him. He asked Gehazi to call the hospitable woman. When she came, he noted her thoughtfulness and asked what he could do for her, even if it meant talking to the king or army commander on her behalf.

Her reply was indicative of her character. Essentially, she noted her contentment. She had no further needs.

After she left the room, Elisha seemed a bit frustrated that he could do nothing for her. Gehazi then mentioned that she had no son. He also pointed out that her husband was old, indicating the unlikeliness of her ever having a child.

Ah! Elisha finally seized on what he could do. He called her again to tell her that by this same time next year, she would be holding a son in her arms.

She could not believe it! Was this man telling the truth? Could it be? Her deepest desire, the thing that all their wealth could not buy, and this man of God had just told her to expect a son next year!

## Joyful Times

I imagine that the next year for her was filled with joyous preparation. A cheerful collecting and making of all things that a baby would need, every item woven and stitched with love and longing.

Then the day came. The rejoicing could hardly be contained. She was happier than she had ever thought possible. The next few years must have flown by for her with pleasant tasks, hugs, and more kisses than imaginable. There was delight in this child.

She surely watched with wonder as he grew. Did she laugh as he first crawled around their rooms, then walked unsteadily, then ran, his chubby legs pumping as he flew through the fields to find his father? What delight she must have had in this precious child of hers and the plans and dreams she had for his future.

## A Desperate Time

But those dreams came to a halt one heart-stopping morning when a servant brought the child, deathly ill, from the field. As she held him, did she tell the servants to bring her this cloth, that herb, more water, trying everything in her power to treat this beloved child? Nothing worked, and she watched and held and prayed until he drew a last breath and lay still on her lap.

I wonder how long she sat there before reality set in, or did she fully realize in an instant that he was gone? Whenever realization came, she knew what to do. With quick steps, she carried the precious son up the stairs to the roof, laid him on Elisha's bed, left the room, shutting the door firmly behind her, and initiated her plan.

Quickly obtaining a donkey and a servant from her

husband, she told him of her intention to visit Elisha but hid the fact of their child's death. Then speedily she set out on her journey to Mt. Carmel and the man of God, knowing that he could bring back her child. Not her husband, not a doctor, not Gehazi, but only God through his prophet Elisha could do that.

Elisha, of course, listened and acted. When the dead son came back to life, his mother fell at Elisha's feet, bowing to the ground, in gratitude and praise to God. This miracle performed by God through Elisha is a beautiful illustration of God's power over life and death. Wow! What an ending! Except ... it was not the end.

## God's Care

At some point it seems the woman became a widow since her husband is not mentioned again in the scriptures, and she stood in his place as head of household. While the son was still young enough to be at home, a great famine came to the land. Elisha talked only to her about taking her household to another land that did not have a famine. She listened to the man of God and moved to the land of the Philistines. She and her household were not able to travel home until seven years later when the famine was over.

Upon her return, she discovered that someone else had taken over her land and house. As head of her family, she needed to appeal to King Jehoram to have her property restored.

*Coincidentally,* at the exact moment she entered the king's chamber to petition him for her land, Gehazi, Elisha's servant, was answering the king's request to tell him about Elisha's great deeds. Gehazi *just happened* to be talking about the incident of Elisha restoring life to the Shunammite woman's son. What timing!

Gehazi saw the woman and her son come into the chamber, and introduced her to the king. He then presented the son to the king. "This young man," he likely said, "is the very one I have just described, the same one who has been raised from the dead by Elisha." The king perhaps had been amazed by the account Gehazi told. But seeing the actual mother and son from Gehazi's account standing in front of him, at that very moment, surely caused him to exclaim with delight.

Of course, the king was going to hear this woman's request. And, of course, he answered the request with abundance. He restored the house and land that were rightfully hers. And he gave her all the income that the land had produced during the past seven years. Quite a restoration!

## Coincidence?

I don't believe in coincidence, but I strongly believe in God's providence. As numerous scriptures tell us, God provides for His own (see Ps 37:25–26, 39–40; 2 Cor 9:8–10; 1 Pet 5:7). Through her hospitality, this woman demonstrated her *respect* for God's prophet. By turning to Elisha when her deep need came, she showed her *belief* in God's power through his servant. When she moved from her land, she *obeyed* God's words given through Elisha without question. God cared and provided for this woman and her son.

## Her Appeal for Other Women

This woman in the shadows appeals in so many ways to the hearts of women in varying circumstances. Women who love the proclaimers of God's word are drawn to her for her dedicated care of God's prophet. Women who give "hints" of good ideas to their husbands smile at her suggestion to her husband about a guest room to house Elisha. Childless women who have long desired to be mothers admire her for her calm acceptance of a difficult life circumstance. All those who have been blessed by God with a heart's desire gift understand the elation she must have felt upon receiving such a gift. And those who have experienced deep sorrow empathize with the intensity of her distress at the loss of that great gift.

Her open hospitality, her persistence in finding the one person who could appeal to his God to bring life to her son, and her determined faith that God can do all things serve as examples to all of us. Elisha must have loved and admired her also, for he seemed to be completely at ease in her hospitable household.

## What Can I Learn from
## The Hospitable Woman?

About hospitality? (See also Heb 13:2 and 1 Pet 4:9)

About contentment with current circumstances? (See also Phil 4:11–13 and 1 Tim 6:6–8)

About persistence? (See also Gal 6:9 and Phil 3:13–14)

* * *

### To Think About

Specify a time that hospitality by you, or by someone you know, has led to an enduring relationship.

What can be outcomes for someone who displays discontentment?

Can you think of someone who has displayed contentment even under difficult circumstances? What have you observed about the outcomes of that contentment?

What are other scriptural examples of someone's persistence accomplishing a good outcome?

# Chapter 9

## *The Chronically Ill Woman*

Scripture Texts: Matthew 9:20–22; Mark 5:25–34;
Luke 8:43–48

*So many people! She had not realized the crowd would be so large!
She pulled her head covering closer in front so that it hid most of her
face. Her heart beat faster at the thought of someone recognizing her
and crying out to the others.*

*When she left her house this morning, tired even after a full night's
sleep, she knew she would be breaking the law and that she could be
severely punished, but she also knew that after 12 years of fatigue and
"uncleanness," the Teacher was her only hope. Doctors had been useless,
taking her money while doing little to cure her. In fact, she was getting
worse, not better.*

*The people were crowding together, jostling to get a better view
and moving ahead of each other to be closer to Him. From the
outskirts of the crowd, she couldn't even see where He was.*

*Making sure someone in the crowd did not brush against her, she
stood on tiptoe to get a better view. There he was just ahead where
the crowd was thick! He was talking to an important man who
looked very sad. If only she could get near the Teacher!*

*She managed to move along quickly at the edge of the crowd of followers. Pulling her clothes tightly around her lest they contaminate others, she inched forward into the densest gathering of people. Suddenly, she heard his voice. "Oh, there He is!" she silently cried to herself. "I must get closer!"*

*Her heart began to race when she caught sight of the back of his head. His voice was louder now—talking to and teaching the people. Finally, she saw an opening in the crowd just behind Him. Tentatively, she slowly reached out a hand. Bending slightly at the waist, she was able to finger the fringe of his garment.*

*At once, she felt—different, stronger and whole. Sudden joy filled her heart! She knew without a doubt that she was cured, and she started to move away quickly. Twelve long years and in an instant, it was over! But wait! He's turning around.*

*Her face was hot and she trembled with fear. "Oh, no, no, no! He couldn't have felt that, could he? I did not even touch Him. I know I did not touch Him."*

*The Teacher looked around at the crowd and spoke. "Who touched me?" He asked. His disciples looked at Him in astonishment for the crowd pressed against Him.*

*Shame and humiliation filled her heart. She could hide no longer. Trembling, she fell at His feet.*

\* \* \*

Chronic illness. What a strain it is on anyone who suffers from it! The chronically ill woman in this account had been drained of health and money for 12 years, and her condition grew worse. She knew her only hope was Jesus, the great healer and teacher.

## Difficulties Created by Her Condition?

This woman in the shadows had a discharge of blood (like a menstrual cycle but continuous) for 12 years. Today this is known as menorrhagia.[1]

To understand better how this chronic illness impacted her life, read Leviticus 15:19–28. If she and her household were keepers of the law, and we can only assume they were, her illness affected her not only physically but socially, emotionally, mentally, and spiritually.

As a result of long years of continuous bleeding, she may have suffered from anemia with its resulting tiredness and lack of energy. She may also have had abdominal pain.[2] And there may have been other symptoms of her chronic illness. With its unknown cause and lack of proper treatment, her illness surely preyed on her mind and kept her in emotional turmoil, perhaps even depressed.

As keepers of the law, everyone in her household would have been involved in a constant cycle of events to keep the uncleanness at bay, i.e., constant bathing and washing of clothes and bed linens. They would have been quarantined for a time from others.

Besides suffering socially, she was also separated spiritually. She could not meet with fellow worshippers, for she would have been considered unclean as long as she had the discharge.

So, physically, this woman felt poorly. Emotionally, she was spent. Socially, she was isolated. Mentally, she was exhausted. And I wonder if her spiritual candle seemed dimmer.

## Renewed Hope

This suffering woman lived with dwindling hope for 12 long years. Her hope must have been renewed as she heard rumors about the teachings of Jesus and about His healing of all kinds of diseases and disorders. Perhaps she had stood far away from the crowds as He spoke. Perhaps hope blossomed as she began to believe that His words were true and right and that He was the prophesied Messiah, or perhaps she had glimpsed Jesus as He healed a leper or another "unclean" person like herself. By whatever way she knew about Jesus, what she knew, without a doubt, was that He could heal her even by the slightest touch of the hem of his garment.

## Fringes of a Garment

God had given a commandment to the Israelites to sew tassels on the corners of their garments with a blue cord on each tassel (Num 15:37–40). The tassels were to remind them of the law and their commitment to obeying His commands. We can assume, that as a keeper of the Jewish law, Jesus had tassels on the corners of His outer garment. By touching the tassel or hem, the chronically ill woman seems to indicate she knew the law and the significance of commitment and obedience to God.

## "Who Touched Me?"

Accounts in both Mark and Luke mention the large crowd pressing around Jesus. Luke even notes that the people almost crushed Him. So, when Jesus asked, "Who touched me?" the disciples seemed to be astonished. Can you see them looking at each other with eyebrows raised in silent expressions of "Is He joking? In this crowd?"

But Jesus knew that power had gone out of Him. When He asked the question, he was referring to someone who had been healed.

Wait a minute! Didn't Jesus, as God the Omniscient,

know all things? Did He not know who had touched Him? Of course, He did. Then why did you think He asked the question?

The scriptures do not tell us the answer to that question. But, perhaps, one reason He asked was that the healing would become publicly known. Reluctantly, trembling and fearful, the woman came forth. Kneeling before Him, perhaps expecting condemnation and dismissal because He was now considered unclean by her touch, she confessed everything to Him and, by doing so, to those who were listening.

Why would Jesus allow this poor woman, already ashamed and humiliated by her condition, to suffer through a confession in front of a large crowd? Of course, no reason has been revealed, but consider the following.

The woman's uncleanness was widely known by her neighbors and by other villagers. That knowledge was necessary in order for the townspeople to keep themselves "clean." One commentary noted that if she even touched the clothes of a person, that person would be "ceremonially unclean the rest of the day."[3] But Jesus interacted with her, anyway. Since her uncleanness was public knowledge, perhaps He wanted the knowledge of her healing to be public also.

The healing had produced no visible results. She was not lame but could now walk or blind but could now see. When Jesus asked a question, the answer allowed the woman to recount the "whole truth," as Mark indicated, about the instant healing that occurred. Those who knew her well could see the vitality and strength that had been returned. Her healing was now public knowledge.

Hearing the woman describe her long illness with its heartache and isolation surely touched many hearts and evoked compassion from the crowd. They could be glad with her because she had been healed instantly. She was no longer unclean. She could look forward to a brighter future. Her shame and humiliation became joy and thanksgiving. And it was all because of the Teacher and Healer.

## A Peaceful Freedom

This woman had great faith in Jesus's ability to heal her, and His first words to her noted that. He stated that her faith had healed her.

His next words must have been as soothing to her as ointment on a wound, the comforting and hopeful words she had yearned to hear for 12 years. "Be freed from your suffering."

She was already free from the physical illness, but now she could be free from the mental, emotional, and spiritual distress that the illness caused. She could be with her family again without restrictions. If she had no family, she could now look forward to a husband and children. She could visit neighbors. She could be together with other worshippers at the synagogue. She was free!

## Concluding Thoughts

What a roller coaster of emotions this woman experienced when she encountered Jesus! In just a few seconds, she went from deep sorrow about her condition to intense joy at being healed.

Then the deep fear and humiliation she felt at being discovered turned to relief and joy again at Jesus's words. She learned what millions have discovered—any encounter with Jesus can be life-altering.

## What Can I Learn from
## The Chronically Ill Woman

About persistence in seeking Jesus? (See also Deut 4:29 and Ps 119:10)

About faith in Jesus? (See also Rom 3:21, 22 and 10:17)

* * *

## To Think About

Do you or a family member have a chronic illness? How is the illness life-limiting?

What kind of illnesses today would limit a person's interactions with others? How did you fare with the isolation that came with the 2020 pandemic?

When Jesus healed people, He healed them immediately. How are those miracles different from the healing that today's faith healers purport to do?

Name someone in your congregation or community who has a chronic illness and suggest ways to help and encourage them, and then follow through with the suggestions.

# Chapter 10

## *The Humble Woman*

Scripture Texts: Matthew 15:21–28; Mark 7:24–30

*Her heart swelled with joy! She cried out, "Could it be?" A sudden fear seized her, "Will he be gone already? Oh, no, no, no!" She ran faster "I must hurry, I must hurry, I must hurry!"*

*At daybreak when she had gone to the well to draw water for the day, all the women were chattering noisily. They usually were, but today there was a new level of excitement. "Have you heard?" they greeted her. At her quizzical look, her closest friend blurted, "The Healer is coming!"*

*"Do you mean ...?" she started.*

*"Yes!" said her friend, interrupting her. "The same one we have heard about who heals the lame and blind! He's on the way here—to Tyre and Sidon!"*

*Afraid to believe it was true, she grasped the young woman's arm and asked, "But, how do you know that?!*

*Her friend turned away from the others to face her and answered more softly, "My brother was on the way home from Galilee when he was overtaken in the path by many who were running and shouting.*

*They stopped at every village to tell them that Jesus was coming. Soon my brother met scores of sick and diseased ones being carried to the Healer."*

*At the look of joy and hope that sprang to her friend's eyes, she said carefully, "Perhaps this is something you need to know?"*

*Grasping the young woman's arm more tightly, with the beginning of hope in her eyes she nodded toward the others and said firmly, "They are excited because they think they will see tricks. But I have told you again and again, no one can do what they say he has done without being from God. He can heal my daughter! I know it!"*

*Her friend looked at her for a long time, as if searching for something, then said quietly, "Go! I will draw water for you and look in on your daughter when I take it to your house."*

*Hearing the love and compassion in the friend's voice, she gave her a quick hug, starting to say something, but the woman pushed her away, saying, "Go now! He will be gone if you wait around any longer."*

*She gathered her skirts and took off down the path, glancing back only once with a wide smile of delight. Her friend heard her mutter as she ran, "He's coming, He's coming, He's coming!"*

## Excitement!

What excitement Jesus generated! He spoke with authority. He healed the diseased and demon-possessed. He focused attention on those society shunned. No wonder the vast crowds of common people of Israel and the outlying areas thronged to hear and see Him.

And what mother with a desperately ill child, one whose erratic and violent behavior was caused by a demon, would not cling to the hope Jesus generated? Even if He was a Jew and she was not. Even if her own people might scoff at her for seeking Him.

## To the Land of the Gentiles

At the time of this account, Jesus and His disciples must have been tired. In a short period of time, they had experienced a number of challenging events. They had learned about the death of their friend, John, the baptizer. They had the experience of feeding a crowd of 5,000 men (and many women and children) with a boy's meager lunch of five loaves and two fish.

Those same disciples had then been terrified by a nighttime storm while they were in a boat on the Sea of Galilee. But their terror had turned to amazement when they saw Jesus walking on the water and calming the seas. And they had the ever-present tension from the hypocritical Pharisees and teachers of the law who watched and waited for a punishable word or action from Jesus.

So now, the Great Healer is leading His disciples to a place where they, and He, perhaps can rest away from the crowds. He is leading them northwest of the Sea of Galilee to a largely Gentile area outside Israel known as Phoenician Syria. Mark records that Jesus does not want anyone to know that He is there visiting in a house. But, of course, as the scriptures indicate, Jesus the Son of God cannot be hidden.

## The Crowds

Many people learn of Jesus' presence and clamor to see him. It is noisy as people jostle and shove to be close to Him. Those in need call for Jesus to help them. The blind, the maimed, the sick call His name. One voice, however, dominates. It is the voice of a woman begging Jesus to heal her daughter who is severely tormented by a demon. Jesus does not answer.

She cries out again ... and again ... and again. She cries so loudly and for so long that the disciples have had enough. They beg Jesus to send her away. Jesus's reply to them indicates they probably are asking Jesus to grant her request so that she will leave for He reminds them of His mission. He has been sent only to the lost sheep of the house of Israel.

Who is this woman who is calling for help? Matthew calls her a Canaanite. Mark says she is a Syrophoenician. Both terms clearly indicate she is non-Jewish. She is not of the people chosen by God to bring forth the Savior. She does not have the same knowledge or relationship with God that the Jews have, but ... .

## Jesus Answers

The woman falls at Jesus's feet and begs him with a plaintive cry, "Lord, help me!" Jesus finally answers her. His answer is puzzling to modern ears. In fact, it may sound even rude and uncaring.

Jesus replies to her cry for help by noting that He first needs to feed the children (the lost sheep of Israel). The woman does not argue with Him nor disagree. Her "Yes, Lord" reply indicates she is well aware of Him and His mission.

His next statement, "It is not right to take the children's bread and throw it to the dogs," has created many questions for those giving this passage a cursory reading. At first glance, Jesus's words sound like an insult since the Gentiles were frequently called "dogs," meaning the wild, scavenging animals roaming the countryside.

Dogs may have been considered scavengers in Jewish Palestine "but in well-to-do houses influenced by Greek customs (more familiar to the Syrophoenician woman), dogs were sometimes pets."[1] Pets may have been loved, but they were not members of the household. They did not sit at the table eating a complete meal. Children of the household were the ones who ate a meal at the table while pets ate crumbs that dropped from the family table. The humble woman understood completely.

## The Heart of the Woman

Notice what the woman calls Jesus in Matthew 15:22 and 27. These verses seem to indicate she knows the prophecies that the coming Messiah would be a descendant of David and that she believes Jesus is the Messiah.

Jesus tells her that his primary mission now is to the Jews. Her quick but humble reply indicates she fully understands and is not asking to be fed the same food the Jews are but desires any crumb that drops from the table. She just wants something for her daughter now. She is willing to wait for anything else.

Jesus recognizes her great faith and grants her request. Her daughter is healed immediately.

## Concluding Thoughts

This simple woman with a heart of hope and faith provides a powerful contrast to the Jewish religious leaders. Earlier when Jesus had encountered the Pharisees and law teachers, He quoted a prophecy about them which noted they honored Him with their lips but their hearts were far from Him (Matt 15:7–9; Mark 7:6–8).

Those Pharisees, scribes, and lawyers, purported to be the most knowledgeable in Israel about God's laws, had rejected the One who stood before them. He was the same Messiah prophesied about in the law they knew so well. But this humble woman, who was not an Israelite, believed the prophecies about the Messiah and knew, without doubting, that Jesus was the Messiah with the abundant power to heal her daughter. What a faith!

## What Can I Learn from
## The Humble Woman

About humility? (See also Prov 11:2 and Jas 4:6)


About tenacity? (See also Matt 7:7 and 17:20)


* * *

### To Think About

What do you think is the reason Jesus did not answer the woman's first cries to Him?


How do you think the woman might have felt hearing Jesus say that the children are to be "fed *first*"?


Can you recall witnessing anyone humbling herself in order to do good for another person?


Have you ever moved forward in full faith that your prayer about a difficult situation will be answered? What was the result?

What differences might there be in the life of each of God's children if they truly believed and acted upon the teaching in Matthew 7:7? What differences might there be in your church family if every member acted in faith upon that teaching?

# Chapter 11

## *The Sinful Woman*

### Scripture Text: Luke 7:36–50

*Her heart was hammering as she made her way through the streets. She knew it was partly from fear but mostly from excitement. The Teacher was here! He was at the home of Simon, a leading Pharisee in this village. That fact tempered her excitement somewhat, but then she thought about Him and nothing could extinguish her overwhelming joy.*

*He was different from anyone she had ever seen. The first time she heard Him teaching, she was on the outskirts of the crowd. She dared not move any closer to the men who were ashamed to acknowledge her in the daylight and the women who sneered at her in the marketplace. They would have shunned her completely, not wanting to be close to such a sinful woman.*

*But then the Teacher had looked all the way through the mass of people and straight into her eyes. That's when she felt it. The complete love and understanding He had for her, even with all her debasing sins and the humiliation she felt. He knew her shame but still radiated compassion and love. Unlike anyone she had ever known, this Teacher knew her heart!*

*After that first time, she edged into the crowd when he taught and followed them. He spoke along the way. His message of God's compelling love and His claim to be God's Son reached the hidden recesses of her heart. She grew to have no doubt that He was the promised Messiah, and she loved Him for his love and understanding.*

*When she heard the Teacher would be at a meal at the home of Simon this evening, she determined to do whatever she could to be near Him. But now as she neared the Pharisee's house, her fear rose to the surface.*

*With an understanding born from years of contact with towns-people, she knew what her reception at the home of the Pharisee likely would be. While the laws of hospitality allowed everyone to enter at a banquet for such a guest, even if not to eat, she understood that her welcome from the Pharisee and his friends and neighbors would be cool, at best; perhaps, even hostile.*

*She was willing to risk a cool, even scornful reception, however, because the Teacher would be there. No matter if everyone else shunned her, she harbored a compelling need to express her love and gratitude to the One that she knew came to bring change in lives—in her life.*

*Hugging her gift to Him close to her heart, she felt the prickling of tears. They began to flow as she thought about the love He radiated, His gift to her. Her gift was nothing in comparison to that. She hurried toward the lights of the large house ahead.*

\* \* \*

## Contrasts

What a compelling story of contrasts! On the one hand there is Simon, a Pharisee who is host for the evening. Pharisees emphasized strict obedience to the law and to the multitude of traditions that had grown up around the law. Jesus frequently encountered scorn and disbelief from Pharisees and scribes.

Simon must have been a man of prestige and wealth for hosting a banquet was surely an expensive undertaking. Such a banquet would include invitations to other leaders in the community, and there would be many guests. But ... Simon did not really want to honor Jesus. He wanted to study Him.[1]

On the other hand, there is a poor sinful woman, despised and shunned by those like Simon. She overcame her shame to seek out Jesus at the house of Simon who viewed her as a blatant sinner. Then she humbly provided for Jesus what his host, who had multiple possessions, did not.

## Hospitality

The code of hospitality, based on God's instructions in Leviticus 19:33–34, was strict and binding. Although not mentioned in the scriptures, many expectations were formed around that law and were in use in that culture. Hosts were expected to welcome guests into their homes with a greeting kiss and provide for their needs and comfort. They would arrange to have the feet of their guests washed and often provided oil to be used on head and feet. Both the water and oil provided healing relief to guests after days under the sun on dry and dusty roads. Guests were offered water to drink and a meal to be shared with the host.[2]

On the evening of our account, Simon the host provided only the meal without any welcoming hospitable gestures. By violating the expectations of hospitality, Simon indicated a lack of respect and honor for his guest. He seemed to be saying, "Jesus, you are no more than an interesting teacher and performer."

## Reclining at Table

The phrase "reclining at table" (v 37) indicates that the Jews had adopted the Roman way of dining. Guests would lie on their left sides, resting on their elbows, on small couches arranged around a low table, and would eat with their right hands. Their bare feet would be behind them, pointing away from the table.[3]

## A Sinner's Humble Gift

As Jesus was reclining at Simon's table, an uninvited guest entered the room. A woman of the town, known to everyone as a sinful woman (perhaps a prostitute) entered, clutching an alabaster flask of soothing perfumed oil. Surely every eye in the room zeroed in on her as she made her way toward the guest. She ignored the disapproving looks for she was on a mission. Her gaze was focused on the Teacher.

She knelt behind Jesus at his feet. Perhaps she was overcome with the burden of her sins, or perhaps she noted the absence of expected tokens of welcome for him or perhaps both, for she began to weep. The tears flowed freely as she recalled His love and mercy toward her and others like her.

She cried so many tears that they could have filled a basin. They washed over his tired and dusty feet. The host had provided no drying cloth, but that was of no concern to the woman for she began to wipe Jesus's feet lovingly with her unbound hair. She then repeatedly kissed his feet and poured the fragrant, soothing oil on them and on his head.

## A Sinner's Unrepentant Heart

Simon was incensed by her gestures. A reader can almost visualize his hard stare and disapproving frown. But Simon did not know that his thoughts about this woman, and what her heart had led her to do, revealed two important things about him. First, he did not really believe Jesus was who He said He was ("*If* this man was a prophet ...") and second, he was deceived about his own heart ("he would know what sort of woman this is ... for she is a sinner"). Aghast that his guest would let such a sinful woman touch Him, Simon was blind to his own sin. And Jesus called him on it.

Jesus caught Simon's attention with a parable about two men who had borrowed money from a lender. One owed the equivalent of almost a year and a half of wages. The other had borrowed a sum equal to less than two months of wages. Their moneylender canceled the debt of both. Then Jesus asked Simon a question. Which debtor would have more love for the one who had forgiven the debts?

Simon gave the right answer: The one who loved more would be the one who had the bigger debt canceled. Like a child in a classroom who gives a right answer to a question from his teacher, Simon must have felt proud when Jesus told him he answered correctly. But his pride was about to shatter. He was still blind to his own debt, so Jesus spelled it out for him.

First, Jesus asked a strange question. "Simon, do you see this woman?" Of course, Simon saw the woman. She was in his line of vision. But Jesus may have been asking for Simon to look deeper. Perhaps He was asking, "Simon, do you *really* see this woman? Her burdens, her hopelessness, her despair over her sins, her love and care, and her tender heart? Can you look with compassion at someone with a heart like that? Simon, do you really see her?"

Perhaps also implied by this question is the unspoken one, "Simon, do you see yourself in contrast?" for Jesus offered details to help Simon see more clearly. Simon, Jesus stated, had provided no water with a towel to wash his feet, but the woman had bathed his feet with her tears and toweled them with her hair. Simon had given no welcoming kiss of greeting, but the woman had not ceased to kiss his feet. Simon had neglected to offer oil for Jesus's head, but this "sinner" had bathed his feet with fragrant soothing oil.

Jesus then concluded with a statement to the woman that must have been a lightning bolt to Simon's heart. "Your sins are forgiven." Jesus was canceling her debt! He was canceling the enormous debt of her numerous sins.

## Concluding Thoughts

"Your sins are forgiven." How thrilled the woman must have been to hear those life-refreshing words. While the other guests whispered among themselves about the audacity of Jesus, He turned to the woman and told her that her faith had saved her. Then He gave her a heart-soothing directive, "Go in peace."

Peace! At last, she could have peace. A state of mind and heart that had eluded her for years! The heavy burdens were gone and she could live in hope, in forgiveness, and in peace. And it was all because of Jesus!

## What Can I Learn from
## The Sinful Woman?

About my own compassion toward the burdens of others?
(See also Eph 4:32 and Gal 6:1–2)

About self-righteousness? (See also Rom 12:3 and Gal
6:3–4)

* * *

### To Think About

An alabaster jar of oil was very expensive, worth a year's
wages (see John 12:3–5 for a similar account of another woman
in a different location anointing Jesus). The oil was "not a
typical household oil for anointing, but an expensive perfume
oil used for a solemn and special act of devotion."[4]

Why do you think the sinful woman broke open the seal and
anointed Jesus's feet with the oil? What was she showing by
doing so?

What specific opportunities have you had today to show
compassion to others? Did you take advantage of those
opportunities?

What opportunities have you had this week to honor Jesus? Were you able to do that?


In what specific ways can you regularly assess the state of your heart to be sure no unforgiven sin lurks?


In what ways can you guard against harboring self-righteousness in your heart?

# Chapter 12

## *The Fearful Woman*

### Scripture Text: Matthew 27:11–26

*She cannot stay silent any longer. All day a feeling of dread has surrounded her. She feels physically sick. "Maybe I have a fever," but then she shakes her head. No, this is not sickness.*

*It is the dream. She cannot shake it, this most vivid and appalling dream. She cannot put into words everything that was in the dream, but ever since she awoke with a scream while it was still dark, she has not been able to forget the images. Death and blood and sorrow ... and innocence. They were as real as this hand she raises before her face, shielding herself from the images that assail her.*

*Dread has increased with every hour along with the size of the crowd outside the palace. The priests and elders had gathered first this morning. Then others began to come when word of Jesus's arrest spread through the city. "Will they not stop?" she cries, putting her hands over her ears, as the noise of the crowd penetrates the walls of her room.*

*She knows about this man Jesus that the Jewish priests, elders, and soldiers have now dragged before her husband. Her household has talked of little else for months. All those working in Pilate's palace* speak of what He has done for their people, and how He has healed the blind and the lame and those with leprosy. One of them said her father was one of the thousands that He fed with bread and a few fish from a young boy's lunch. Imagine that! No ordinary person could do that, could he?

They have also talked with her quietly about His teaching, but they have been reluctant to say much. They fear her husband. Jesus' teaching is definitely different from the Roman teachers and even the other Jewish teachers. He speaks of peace and self-control and serving others. "His God is different from the Roman gods," she muses, glancing at the statues around the room. "He says God is living and powerful and above all gods. Not made of clay or wood." Although she prays and shows honor to her gods, she knows deep inside that the lifeless images can do nothing.

As her maids have recounted Jesus' lessons to her, she has caught glimpses of another kind of life. A life given to this one God and filled with helping others is unlike anything she has ever known. "Could a life like that be satisfying," she has wondered more than once, "and is there really a life after this one?" She considers this, remembering what the servant who was helping her dress told her just two days ago.

"Enough of this!" she says decisively, rising from the seat. "I must warn Pilate!" she mutters aloud. "I know he is about to do something terrible—and wrong! He is about to condemn an innocent man!"

Mumbling half to herself with broken words and sobbing at the dread she feels, she moves swiftly to the door, calling for a servant to come quickly. If she sends a message now, perhaps her husband will listen. He must make the right decision!

\* \* \*

## A Dream

Terrified! In agony and dread! And all from a heart-racing dream about Jesus. What a dream that must have been!

Matthew records four times that God sent dreams to people. Three of those dreams were sent to Joseph to protect Jesus from Herod, and the other one was sent to re-route the wise men of the East after their journey to see the infant Jesus. So, sometimes God communicated important information to certain persons in dreams.

We have no information about this dream of the fearful woman being from God, but dreams were important to many ancient civilizations including the Romans. In her doctoral dissertation about dreams, Juliette Harrison notes that the reason any culture places value on dreams is that they think they might foretell the future.[1] A dream that upset Pilate's wife as much as it did would most likely be interpreted by her culture to mean that a dreadful event was about to happen.

The scriptures do not indicate the content of her dream, but she was distressed greatly by it. She indicated in the note to her husband that she had "suffered much" from the dream. What does the phrase "suffered much" mean to you? Did it mean the dream interrupted her sleep? Did she awaken in the dark gasping for breath, her heart beating wildly? Or was the dream so disturbing that she could not get the images out of her mind? Did the dream fill her with dread because it indicated a dire event ahead for her or her husband or for both?

We don't know what caused her suffering or what form it took, but we do know her anguish was powerful enough that it moved her to take action. She sent an urgent message begging her husband, who was already seated in the judgment hall to hear the case before him, to have nothing to do with that righteous man Jesus.

I am not sure if sending a message *after* the judge was

seated in the judgment seat was unorthodox for a Roman trial, but it would probably be precedent-setting in most courtrooms today. For her to have no regard for the timing of her message seems to indicate the extremity of her fear. She was terrified that Pilate would be involved in bringing about whatever dreadful things were contained in her dream.

## Who Is the Dreamer?

We are not told anything else about Pilate's wife in scripture or by history but traditions have grown up around this account. The Apocryphal book *The Gospel of Nicodemus* gives her the name Claudia Procula and identifies her as a granddaughter of Augustus, the Roman emperor.[2] Some think she may have been a proselyte to Judaism and a follower of Jesus. The Greek Orthodox Church, considering her to be a saint, honors her each year with a feast day on October 27.[3]

Since she is not named in the scriptures, which is our only source for spiritual truths, we can put no stock in these other accounts. They remain only traditions. Her name and later history are unknown to us.

## That Righteous Man

Pilate's wife warned her husband to have nothing to do with "that righteous man." Think about that for a moment. At the time of this account, the Romans had conquered and were inhabiting Judea and its surrounding areas. They exacted taxes from the Jews and demanded they obey their Roman rulers, causing much friction and provoking underlying rebellion against them. Pilate was the Roman governor of the province of Judea. What are your thoughts on how this man's wife knew that Jesus, politically one of her husband's subjects

and socially an itinerant man of few possessions, was a "righteous man"?

We can only speculate. Did she have friends who had
heard Jesus teach? Was she close to her servants, who may
have been conquered Jews? Did they speak with her about
Jesus? Or did she overhear them, perhaps hiding so they
would not see her? If so, did they recount the miracles He
performed, the healings, the feedings of thousands, and the
divine words of forgiveness? Did they recall in detail the care
and tenderness with which He interacted with the poor and
suffering?

At some point, had she slipped out of her well-guarded
palace and, perhaps in a poor woman's disguise, skirted the
edge of a crowd to hear His words? Or had her Roman friends
recounted the cleansing of the temple, while she sat mute,
secretly admiring His courage? Of course, as much as we
search for answers to these questions, we will find none. The
scriptures are completely silent about the "how".

We only know that this woman from the equestrian
(upper middle) class of Roman society[4] somehow was
convinced that Jesus was a righteous man who did not deserve
to die. And she desperately wanted to convince her husband
of that fact.

## The Accusations

Jewish law specified that death was the consequence of blasphemy (Lev 24:16) which was the first accusation of the
Jewish leaders against Jesus. However, capital punishment
required a decision by the Romans in power. Pilate refused to
condemn Jesus to death for blasphemy, knowing that the
accusation was untrue, stating he found "no fault in him."

The chief priests and scribes quickly found something
that the Roman governor might be concerned about. They

accused Jesus of stating that He was the king of the Jews. They knew this would be interpreted as a direct threat to the Roman emperor, Tiberius, and Pilate definitely did not want to offend the great Tiberius. But any threat to the Roman emperor, the one who had placed him in office as governor, would also be a threat to Pilate's own position of power. Pilate, of course, immediately realized the threats. The pressure was on.

When the mob shouted that Jesus was a Galilean, perhaps hoping he could shift decision-making and mend a relationship, Pilate sent Him to Herod Antipas, the tetrarch of Galilee. Herod was excited because He wanted to see Jesus perform some sign, but when Jesus refused to answer Herod's questions, Herod sent Him back (see Luke 23:6–12).

## Pilate's Indecision/Decision

Even then, Pilate did not find Jesus guilty. He seemed to latch onto something else that could get himself out of decision making. Since it was a custom that an imprisoned criminal was to be released every year during these feast days of the Jews, he gave the Jews a choice. Whom should he release, the hardened criminal Barabbas, or the innocent Jesus?

Barabbas's crimes were not in question. He was an insurrectionist, a murderer, and a robber. He had broken all kinds of laws the Jews were expected to keep. Perhaps Pilate thought this undisputable fact would influence the leaders' decision to allow him to release Jesus. It did not.

Evidently, in their eyes, releasing a criminal was a small thing compared to losing their own power and positions. They remained intent and focused on getting rid of the man who threatened their religious authority and their highly respected places in the Jewish world.

Pilate continued to protest Jesus's innocence. But by this

time, the Jews had found the one thing that seemed to carry weight with Pilate. They told Pilate that if he released Jesus, he was no friend of Caesar. That seemed to be the last straw. Still refusing to condemn Jesus, Pilate caved in to the pressure of the crowd and the threat to his own position.

Pilate called for a basin of water, washed his hands in front of those clamoring for Jesus's death, and declared that he was innocent of that man's blood. He thought he would put the burden of Jesus's death into the hands of the Jews. He had not declared Jesus guilty, but he refused to take a stand against the efforts of the Jews to condemn an innocent man, sealing Jesus's fate. Whether he ever had a fleeting thought about his wife's request is unknown.

## Concluding Thoughts

Pilate refused to make a firm public decision about the fate of Jesus. By his refusal, however, he actually made a decision. By not taking a strong stand when Jewish leaders first led Jesus to him and by his inaction in the face of a lack of evidence, he allowed himself to be complicit with the Jewish people. They put to death a completely innocent and righteous man, which Pilate's wife had feared. The Jewish leaders (and Pilate) murdered the Son of God.

## What Can We Learn from
## The Fearful Woman?

About speaking up in the face of injustice? (See also Mic 6:8; 2 Chron 19:7; Prov 22:8)

About taking firm action to prevent an injustice?

* * *

### To Think About

Can you recall an instance in which someone you know took action to prevent injustice? What was the result?

What examples of injustice do you see in today's world? What can you say or do in response to those injustices?

What can you imagine might have happened in Pilate's household after Jesus was crucified?

# Chapter 13

## *Final Thoughts*

The women in the scriptures we have studied throughout this book are varied in many ways. While they share the distinction of being a part of God's divine book, their depiction in it is not positive in every case. Many of the women are admirable, but some are not. Are you thinking of the conniving woman and the otherworldly woman?

Some display a deep faith in God while others have no relationship with Him, and at least one seems to have little or no knowledge of Him. Although knowing about Him, at least two of the women are openly disobedient to His law and will. Some of the women display little grace, while others act with humble hearts.

## Commonalities

Some commonalities, however, connect them. They are all women, and yet not one is named. They all live in time periods when a woman's predominant role was as wife and mother. Many of them are known, not by name, but by relationship with a male, usually a husband or, in one case, a father. Others are known because of their interactions with men selected by God for distinct service (prophets and kings). All the women selected from the New Testament have some type of connection with Jesus. Three of them seek Him out, either for His healing powers or to honor Him, and the other advocates for His innocence because of her dream.

## Relationships

We know that five of the women were married. The self-sacrificing woman was widowed, and the humble woman was either married at the time the scriptural incident occurred or was widowed.

We do not know if all the women had children. There are references to at least 15 children in five of the accounts. Three of those accounts involve the deaths of twelve children with 3 of them being brought back to life. One additional chapter involves the sickness of a child. The accounts of the conniving woman and the fearful woman, while noting husbands, do not mention children. The accounts of the otherworldly woman, the dramatic woman, the chronically ill woman, and the sinful woman do not mention family members, although all could have been married and could have had children. The resolute young woman was a virgin and would never marry.

## Time Periods

The women from the Old Testament lived in various time periods. Three of the women lived during the time of the patriarchs, although there is some question about the time period for Job's wife. Jephthah's daughter lived during the time of the judges. Two women lived during the time of King Saul and King David, and two others came into contact with God's prophets during the time of the later kings.

The women selected from the New Testament lived during the short time span corresponding to the approximate three years of Jesus's ministry. That means the women in all of these lessons lived in time periods that perhaps stretched over as much as or more than 2,000 years. And yet, their challenges, their concerns, and their actions are still relevant even in today's modern age.

## Social Strata

The women selected for inclusion in this book came from differing social strata. Several were wealthy while at least one was desperately poor. Two others were outside the mainstream of their societies. The otherworldly woman practiced the black arts prohibited by God and her society, and the sinful woman from the New Testament had been engaged in activities obviously frowned upon by her culture. Both the self-sacrificing woman and the humble woman were from regions slightly outside the area and culture of Israel.

Two of the women lived in a completely different culture from God's people. Potiphar's wife lived in a wealthy household in Egypt, while Pilate's wife made her home among the equestrian society (upper middle class) of the Roman Empire.

## Challenges

Each woman in this series faced a challenge of some sort. Job's wife faced the suffering that severe losses bring and the intense aftereffects of those losses. Lot's wife reacted to the sudden loss of her home and its surrounding city, and

Potiphar's wife ignored understood and stated boundaries. The dramatic woman was challenged by a request to convince her king to change his tactics regarding his estranged son and heir.

The medium of Endor had the challenge of a sinful request by her king, who was asking her to defy his own ruling and the law of God. The resolute young woman had to face a life far different from the one she had always envisioned because of her father's hasty vow. The widow of Zarephath was looking squarely at starvation for herself and her child, and the hospitable woman's great challenge was facing the death of her dearly loved son.

The women who sought out Jesus were facing challenges of their own. One woman had a chronic illness for 12 years and had spent all her money on useless treatment. She was challenged by trying to reach the only one who could heal her illness. The humble woman had to cross an ethnic divide to seek out Jesus who she believed could, and would, heal her daughter. The sinful woman faced shame and humiliation from her countrymen so that she could shower her Savior with honor and esteem. The fearful woman had the challenge of trying to convince her important husband not to get involved in the plot of the Jews crying for the death of an innocent man.

## Responses to Challenges

As the women faced the challenges, their actions and their responses to God and His truths seem to have formed the basis for their inclusion in the scriptures. They met their challenges with differing words and with differing actions. Job's wife met her challenge with despair which prompted her outburst to her husband. The disobedient woman gave in to the desire to look back at what she was leaving instead of looking forward to where God was leading her. The conniving woman met the challenge of Joseph's refusal of her attention with anger and vengeance. The resolute young woman met her challenge with courage and commitment.

The otherworldly woman faced her king's unorthodox request first with hesitancy but then with obedience which involved her in prohibited practices. The dramatic woman cheerfully obeyed Joab's request, prepared well, and approached the king with confidence and assurance. The self-sacrificing woman, facing starvation, nevertheless obediently prepared food and drink for God's prophet. The hospitable woman welcomed the prophet into her home and sought God through him to save her son's life.

A chronically ill woman's faith caused her to defy the letter of the law and the conventions of her society to seek out the only one who could heal her. The humble woman, a Gentile, presented herself before the Jewish teacher, Jesus, to beg for His healing of her daughter. The sinful woman faced the humiliating reproach of townspeople gathered in a house where she was not wanted in order to express her intense gratitude and love for her Savior. The fearful Roman woman sent an urgent message to her husband regarding the innocence of the Jewish prisoner, Jesus.

Each of the women is representative of certain women in any time period and in any society. Some met their trials with courage and faith in God. Others met their challenges without thinking of God, while some were deliberately disobedient to Him.

## Concluding Thoughts

When I began writing this book, my intention was to bring these women out of the shadows. I wanted to shine a spotlight on them so that we women of today could more easily identify with them. It has been almost 2,000 years since the last of the women acted or spoke what God recorded. Those 2,000 years coupled with the approximate 2,000-year span from the first of them to the last indicates that about 4,000 years separate us from the oldest account. Yet their actions and words are contemporary.

The ways they met their trials and temptations are the same ways we meet ours. Their words echo through our own speech. Their trials and challenges are similar to our own, and their faith, or lack of it, moves along a spectrum just as ours does.

As you reflect on the actions and words of these women as recorded in the scriptures, consider the following questions:

1. Which accounts do you remember most vividly and why?
2. Were there any women with whom you identified most readily and why?
3. Which accounts taught you something you did not know previously?
4. Were there any women who inspired you, and if so, by what were you inspired?
5. As these women met their challenges, did you see yourself in the actions or words of any of them?

Nothing in God's word is superfluous. There are no by-the-ways. There is nothing that is irrelevant. The inclusion of these women is not an accident. They lived and breathed, hoped and prayed, loved and were loved, doubted and had faith, just as we do now.

I hope they have come alive for you and that perhaps their

lives have been in full color instead of black and white. I pray that they will continue to live for you.

I also hope that you can see the kinship of these women with those of us living today and that you will continue to be inspired by the ones who acted with intense faith. There is much to be learned from these women in the shadows.

# Notes

## 1. The Despairing Woman

1.  A.W. Tozer, *The Knowledge of the Holy* (New York: HarperCollins, 1961), 1.
2.  Tozer, *The Knowledge of the Holy*, 3.

## 3. The Conniving Woman

1.  James Bronson Reynolds, "Sex, Morals and the Law in Ancient Egypt and Babylon," *Journal of Criminal Law and Criminology*, 5.1 art 4, 1914. http://scholarlycommons.law.northwestern.edu/cgi/viewcontent.cgi?article=1277&context=jclc. Accessed 22 June 2018.
2.  John H. Walton, Victor H. Matthews, and Mark W. Chavalas, *The IVP Bible Background Commentary: Old Testament* (Downers Grove, IL: Inter-Varsity Press, 2000), 71.
3.  Alfred Edersheim, *Bible History: Old Testament,* (Peabody, MA: Hendrickson, 1995), 105.

## 4. The Resolute Young Woman

1.  Adam Clarke, *Clarke's Commentary,* vol 2, Joshua-Esther, (Nashville, TN: Abingdon Press, n.d.), 149.
2.  Wayne Jackson, "What About Jephthah's Vow?", *Christian Courier.* http://www.christiancourier.com/articles/1081-what-about-jephthah's-vow. Accessed June 15, 2022.
3.  Leon Wood, *A Survey of Israel's History* (Grand Rapids, MI: Zondervan, 1970), 224.
4.  Eugene Merrill, *An Historical Survey of the Old Testament* (Nutley, NJ: Craig Press, 1966), 176.
5.  Merrill, *Historical Survey*, 176.

# 5. The Otherworldly Woman

1. Alfred Edersheim, *Bible History: Old Testament* (Peabody, MA: Hendrickson, 1995), 504.
2. Donald Regan, *For the Record: From Wall Street to Washington* (San Diego: Harcourt, 1988), 3.
3. http://www.dictionary.com/divination. Accessed June 22, 2022.
4. http://www.dictionary.com/necromancer. Accessed June 22, 2022.
5. http://www.yourdictionary.com/medium/noun. Accessed June 22, 2022.

# 9. The Chronically Ill Woman

1. https://mayoclinic.org/diseasesandconditions/m/menstrualbleedingexcessive/menorrhagia/complication. Accessed June 14, 2022.
2. https://my.clevelandclinic.org/diseasesandconditions/menorrhagia/symptomsandcauses. Accessed June 14, 2022.

# 10. The Humble Woman

1. Craig S. Keener, *The Bible Background Commentary: New Testament* (Downers Grove, IL: IVP Academic, 2014), 154.

# 11. The Sinful Woman

1. James Burton Coffman, *Luke,* James Burton Coffman Commentaries 3 (Abilene, TX: ACU Press, 1975), 146.
2. Ralph Gower, *The New Manners and Customs of Bible Times* (Chicago: Moody Press 1987), 245.
3. Gower, *The New Manners and Customs of Bible Times*, 246–247.
4. Clinton Arnold, *Zondervan Illustrated Bible Backgrounds Commentary* (Grand Rapids, MI: Zondervan, 1984), 1:161.

# 12. The Fearful Woman

1. Juliette Grace Harrison, *Dreams and Dreaming in the Roman Empire: Cultural Memory and Imagination,* Thesis submitted for the degree of Doctor of Philosophy, (University of Birmingham, Institute of Archeology and Antiquity, College of Arts and Law, September 2001). http//:www.etheses.bham.ac.uk. Accessed August 16, 2021.

2. Edith Deen, *All the Women of the Bible* (New York: Harper & Row, 1955), 207.

3. Herbert Lockyer, *The Women of the Bible* (Grand Rapids, MI: Zondervan, 1967), 226–227.

4. J. D. Douglas, ed., *The Illustrated Bible Dictionary* (Leicester, England: InterVarsity Press, 1994), 3:1229.

# Bibliography

Arnold, Clinton. *Zondervan Illustrated Bible Backgrounds Commentary*. Grand Rapids, MI: Zondervan, 1984.

Beck, John A., *Everyday Life in Bible Time*. Grand Rapids, MI: Baker, 2013.

Boles, H. Leo. *A Commentary on the Gospel According to Matthew*. Nashville, TN: Gospel Advocate, 1967.

Buttrick, John Arthur, ed. *The Interpreter's Bible*. New York: Abingdon Press, 1951.

Carter, Warren. *The Roman Empire and the New Testament: An Essential Guide*. Nashville, TN: Abingdon Press, 2006.

Adam Clarke. *Clarke's Commentary*. Nashville, TN: Abingdon Press, n.d.

Coffman, James Burton. *Luke,* James Burton Coffman Commentaries 3. Abilene, TX: ACU Press, 1975.

Deen, Edith. *All the Women of the Bible*. New York: Harper & Row, 1955.

Dever, William G. *The Lives of Ordinary People in Ancient Israel: Where Archeology and the Bible Intersect*. Grand Rapids, MI: Eerdmans, 2012.

Douglas, J. D., ed. *The Illustrated Bible Dictionary*. Leicester, England: InterVarsity Press, 1994.

Edersheim, Alfred. *Bible History: Old Testament*. Peabody, MA: Hendrickson, 1995.

Evans, Craig A. and Stanley E. Porter, eds. *Dictionary of New Testament Background*. Downers Grove, IL: InterVarsity Press, 2000.

Goodman, Martin. *Rome and Jerusalem: The Clash of Ancient Civilizations.* New York: Alfred A. Knopf, 2007.

Gower, Ralph. *The New Manners and Customs of Bible Times.* Chicago: Moody Press 1987.

Green, Joel B., Scot McKnight, and I. Howard Marshall, eds. *Dictionary of Jesus and the Gospels.* Downers Grove, IL: InterVarsity Press, 1992.

Keener, Craig S. *The Bible Background Commentary: New Testament.* Downers Grove, IL: IVP Academic, 2014.

Kelso, James L. *Archaeology and the Ancient Text.* Grand Rapids, MI: Zondervan, 1968.

Lockyer, Herbert. *The Women of the Bible.* Grand Rapids, MI: Zondervan, 1967.

Merrill, Eugene. *An Historical Survey of the Old Testament.* Nutley, NJ: Craig Press, 1966.

Packer, J. I. and M. C. Tenney, eds. *Illustrated Manners and Customs of the Bible.* Nashville, TN: Thomas Nelson, 1980.

Richards, Sue and Larry Richards. *Every Woman in the Bible.* Nashville, TN: Thomas Nelson, 2003.

Regan, Donald. *For the Record: From Wall Street to Washington.* San Diego: Harcourt, 1988.

Roberts, Jenny. *Bible Then and Now.* Edison, NJ: Chartwell, 1996.

Simmons, William A. *Peoples of the New Testament World.* Peabody, MA: Hendrickson Publishers, 2008.

Stevens, William Arnold and Ernest DeWitt Burton. *Harmony of the Gospels.* New York: Charles Scribner's Sons, 1932.

Stroubal, Eugene. *Life of the Ancient Egyptians*. Norman, OK: University of Oklahoma Press, 1992.

Tenney, Merrill C. *New Testament Times*. Grand Rapids, MI: Eerdmans, 1965.

Tozer, A. W. *The Knowledge of the Holy*. New York: HarperCollins, 1961.

Walton, John H., Victor H. Matthews, and Mark W. Chavalas. *The IVP Bible Background Commentary: Old Testament*. Downers Grove, IL: Inter-Varsity Press, 2000.

Wood, Leon. *A Survey of Israel's History*. Grand Rapids, MI: Zondervan, 1970.

**On-line References**

Butt, Kyle, "Does God Accept Human Sacrifice?" *Apologetics Press*. http://www.apologeticspress.org/articles. Accessed May 5, 2022.

Butt, Kyle, "Jesus, the Syrophoenician Woman, and Little Dogs," *Apologetics Press*. http://www.apologeticspress.org./articles. Accessed October 18, 2017.

Carey, "Jesus and the Syrophoenician Woman: A Case Study in Inclusiveness." Pepperdine Digital Commons, 2011. http://digitalcommonspepperdine.edu/cgi/viewcontent.cgi?article=1104&context=leaven. Accessed October 18, 2017.

Darling, Daniel, "The Most Misunderstood Woman in the Bible," *Today's Christian Woman*, 2011. http://www.todayschristianwoman.com/articles/2011/may/mostmisunderstood,html. Accessed June 17, 2015.

Harrison, Juliette Grace. *Dreams and Dreaming in the Roman Empire: Cultural Memory and Imagination*. Thesis submitted for the degree of Doctor of Philosophy. (University of Birmingham, Institute of Archeology and Antiquity, College of Arts and Law, September 2001). http//:www.etheses.bham.ac.uk. Accessed August 16, 2021.

Higgs, Liz, "Bad Girls of the Bible," Liz Curtis Higgs.com. https://www.l-izcurtishiggs.com/bad-girls-of-the-bible-potiphars-wife/#sthash.rWv-QKbiX.dpuf. Accessed June 22, 2018.

Jackson, Jason. "The Syrophoenician Woman: A Woman of Great Faith." *The Christian Courier.* https://www.christiancourier.com/articles/1235-syrophoenician-woman-a-woman-of-great-faith-the. Accessed October 19, 2017.

Jackson, Wayne. "Mrs. Job—A Portrait of Defection." *The Christian Courier.* https://www.christiancourier.com/articles/491-mrs-job-a-portrait-of-defection. Accessed June 23, 2015.

Jackson, Wayne. "What About Jephthah's Vow?" *Christian Courier.* http://www.christiancourier.com/articles/1081-what-about-jephthah's-vow. Accessed June 15, 2022.

Lyons, Eric. "When Did Job Live?" *Apologetics Press,* July 3, 2008. https://www.apologeticspress.org/articles/doctrinalmatters. Accessed April 25, 2022.

Miller, Dave. "Jephthah's Daughter," *Apologetics Press,* August 2013. https://www.apologeticspress.org/articles. Accessed April 25, 2022.

Overholt, Thomas W. "Medium of Endor: Bible." *Shalvi/Hyman Encyclopedia of Jewish Women.* 31 December 1999. https://wa.org/encyclopedia/article/medium-of-endor-bible>. Accessed June 29, 2022.

Reiss, Moshe. "Jephthah's Daughter." *Jewish Bible Quarterly.* 37.1, 2009, 58–63. https://jbq,jewishbible.org. Accessed June 2, 2022.

Reynolds, James Bronson. "Sex, Morals and the Law in Ancient Egypt and Babylon." *Journal of Criminal Law and Criminology,* 5.1 art 4, 1914. http://scholarlycommons.law.northwestern.edu/cgi/viewcontent.cgi?article=1277&context=jclc. Accessed 22 June 2018.

Shive, Rickey, "The Shunammite Woman," Hickory College Church of Christ, Shade, KY.

https://www.sermoncentral.com/sermons/the-shunammite-woman-rickey-shive-sermon-on-ot-characters-44425-asp?Page=3. Accessed June 22, 2018.

# Scripture Index

**Old Testament**

**Genesis**

| | |
|---|---|
| 2:24 | 23 |
| 12:4–9 | 12 |
| 13:10–13 | 11 |
| 19 | 10 |
| 19:4 | 12 |
| 19:16–26 | 13 |
| 19:30 | 16 |
| 37 | 19 |
| 39:1–23 | 17 |
| 39:7 | 19 |
| 39:20 | 21 |
| 39:22 | 22 |

**Exodus**

| | |
|---|---|
| 21:15 | 31 |

**Leviticus**

| | |
|---|---|
| 15:19–28 | 67 |
| 18:9 | 47 |
| 18:21 | 31 |
| 19:31 | 37, 39 |
| 19:33–34 | 82 |
| 20:1–5 | 31 |
| 20:6 | 37 |
| 20:7 | 39 |
| 20:8 | 39 |
| 20:26 | 39 |
| 20:27 | 37, 39 |
| 24:13–16 | 4 |
| 24:16 | 92 |
| 24:17 | 45 |

**Numbers**

| | |
|---|---|
| 15:37–40 | 68 |
| 30:1–2 | 31 |
| 35:30–34 | 45 |

**Deuteronomy**

| | |
|---|---|
| 4:29 | 71 |
| 12:31 | 31 |
| 18:9–14 | 37 |
| 18:10–13 | 31 |

| | |
|---|---|
| 19:11–13 | 46 |
| 22:28–29 | 47 |
| 23:21–23 | 31 |

**Judges**

| | |
|---|---|
| 11 | 25 |
| 11:30–31 | 30–31 |
| 11:39 | 32 |

**1 Samuel**

| | |
|---|---|
| 15 | 36 |
| 15:22 | 16, 39 |
| 15:23 | 39 |
| 15:27 | 38 |
| 17:47 | 34 |
| 28:3–25 | 35 |

**2 Samuel**

| | |
|---|---|
| 3:2–4 | 48 |
| 3:3 | 45 |
| 5:14 | 48 |
| 13 | 43 |
| 13:20 | 43 |
| 13:21 | 44 |
| 13:37 | 44 |
| 13:39 | 45 |
| 14:1–20 | 41 |
| 18:33 | 48 |

**1 Kings**

| | |
|---|---|
| 1:5–6 | 44 |
| 16:33 | 52 |
| 17:8–24 | 50 |
| 17:12 | 55 |
| 17:18 | 55 |
| 17:24 | 55 |

**2 Kings**

| | |
|---|---|
| 4:8–37 | 57 |
| 8:1–6 | 57 |

**1 Chronicles**

| | |
|---|---|
| 21:11–12 | 31 |

**2 Chronicles**

| | |
|---|---|
| 19:7 | 95 |
| 20:15 | 34 |

**Job**

| | |
|---|---|
| 1–2:10 | 1 |
| 1:5 | 4 |
| 1:11 | 4 |
| 2 | 4 |
| 2:3–5 | 4 |
| 7 | 4 |
| 19 | 4 |
| 42 | 6 |
| 42:10–17 | 6 |

**Psalms**

| | |
|---|---|
| 34:17–19 | 8 |
| 37:25–26 | 62 |
| 37:39–40 | 62 |
| 56:3 | 8 |
| 56:4 | 8 |
| 119:10 | 71 |
| 119:37 | 15 |
| 119:67 | 8 |
| 119:71 | 8 |

**Proverbs**

| 11:2 | 78 |
| 22:8 | 95 |

**Ecclesiastes**

| 9:10 | 49 |

**Jeremiah**

| 7:23–24 | 34 |

**Ezekiel**

| 16:49–50 | 12 |

**Micah**

| 6:8 | 95 |


**New Testament**

**Matthew**

| 7:7 | 78–79 |
| 9:20–22 | 65 |
| 15:7–9 | 76 |
| 15:21–28 | 72 |
| 15:22 | 76 |
| 15:27 | 76 |
| 17:20 | 78 |
| 19:5–6 | 23 |
| 27 | xix |
| 27:11–26 | 88 |
| 27:19 | xix |

**Mark**

| 5:25–34 | 65 |
| 7:6–8 | 76 |
| 7:24–30 | 72 |

**Luke**

| 4:25–26 | 56 |
| 7:36–50 | 80 |
| 7:37 | 83 |
| 8:43–48 | 65 |
| 9:62 | 16 |
| 23:6–12 | 93 |

**John**

| 12:3–5 | 86 |

**Acts**

| 10:34–35 | 56 |

**Romans**

| 3:21 | 71 |
| 3:22 | 71 |
| 6:16 | 16 |
| 10:17 | 71 |
| 12:3 | 86 |
| 13:1–5 | 49 |

**2 Corinthians**

| 1:3 | 8 |
| 1:4 | 8 |
| 1:8–10 | 8 |
| 9:8–10 | 62 |

**Galatians**

| 6:1–2 | 86 |
| 6:3–4 | 86 |
| 6:9 | 64 |

**Ephesians**

| 4:32 | 86 |

5:31–33      23

**Philippians**

3:13–14      64
4:11–13      64

**Colossians**

3:11      56
3:23–24      49

**1 Timothy**

5:17      49
5:19      49
6:6–8      64

**Hebrews**

12:3–4      56
13:2      64
13:17      49

**James**

4:6      78
4:10      34
5:10–11      56

**1 Peter**

4:9      64
5:6      8
5:7      8, 62

**2 Peter**

2:20–22      16

**1 John**

3:18      8
5:3      34

# About the Author

Dr. Betty Hamblen (PhD, Texas Woman's University) has served as Public Relations Director, professor, and board member with Heritage Christian University. Her career has included work in hospitals as the Director of Education and Training and as a mental health counselor. She and husband, Willie, continue active lives in ministry.

# Also by Cypress Publications

*Always Near: Listening for Lessons from God*
by Bill Bagents

*The Christian Life: Chapters for Bible Teacher*
by Ed Gallagher

*Cruciform Christ: 52 Reflections on the Gospel of Mark*
by Travis Bookout

*Easing Life's Hurts* 2nd ed.
by Jack Wilhelm and Bill Bagents

*Equipping the Saints: A Practical Study of Ephesians 4:11–16*
by Bill Bagents and Cory Collins

*The Holy Spirit: A Bible Study Guide*
by Jack Wilhelm

*Jesus the Christ: Chapters for Bible Teachers*
by Ed Gallagher

*King of Glory: 52 Reflections on the Gospel of John*
by Travis Bookout

*Rescue: God and Sin in the Old Testament*
by John F. Wakefield

*Revisiting Life's Oases: Soul-Soothing Stories*
by Bill Bagents

*Welcoming God's Word: Reading with Head and Heart*
by Bill Bagents

*WHAM! Facing Life's Heavy Hits: Thirteen Old Testament Encounters*

By Bill and Laura S. Bagents

*WHAM! Facing Life's Heavy Hits: Thirteen New Testament Encounters*

By Bill and Laura S. Bagents

CYPRESS

To see full catalog of Heritage Christian University Press and
its imprint Cypress Publications, visit
www.hcu.edu/publications